RELEVANT KNOWLEDGE SERIES

Service Quality

VALARIE A. ZEITHAML
A. PARASURAMAN

MARKETING SCIENCE INSTITUTE
Cambridge, Massachusetts

Contents

Electronic Service Quality

Figure

Foreword

The Relevant Knowledge Series, published by the Marketing Science Institute, was established to fill a need for high-quality, detailed books on important business topics. The first two books in the series, *Sales Promotion* by Scott Neslin and *Branding and Brand Equity* by Kevin Lane Keller, focus on areas of longstanding management concern and research interest. Similarly, *Service Quality* addresses a topic of critical business importance and considerable academic attention.

Authors Valarie Zeithaml and A. Parasuraman are uniquely qualified to offer an overview of existing and new knowledge in this area. Since the mid-1980s, when service quality emerged as an important component of services marketing, their research has been pivotal in defining the construct of service quality and developing ways to measure and improve service performance. Indeed, SERVQUAL, the dominant approach to measuring service quality, was developed by Zeithaml and Parasuraman and co-author Leonard Berry nearly two decades ago and continues to be widely used today.

In *Service Quality*, Zeithaml and Parasuraman offer readers a rigorous and practical overview of service quality: how to define it, how to measure it, and how to improve service performance. They also discuss growing evidence of the strong links between service quality, customer loyalty, and profitability, and the still-emerging challenges of delivering quality service via the Internet.

Service quality is a concern that crosses industries and sectors; likewise *Service Quality* will appeal to a broad cross-section of readers. Academic researchers will find a detailed survey of two decades' research as well as an outline of important unanswered questions. Managers will find a practical overview of how to understand, measure, and improve service performance and measurement tools for use in their own firms. We hope that all readers find something that informs, guides, and inspires their work in this important area.

Leigh M. McAlister
University of Texas at Austin
MSI Executive Director 2003–05

ACKNOWLEDGEMENTS

A shorter version of this monograph appears in *Handbook of Marketing*, edited by Robin Wensley and Barton Weitz, published by Sage Publications. Appreciation is extended to the Marketing Science Institute and its member companies for sponsoring much of the research in this monograph and to Leonard L. Berry, our co-author of twenty years on the topic of service quality.

Valarie Zeithaml
University of North Carolina at Chapel Hill

A. Parasuraman
University of Miami

Executive Summary

Service quality has become a key marketing tool for achieving competitive differentiation and fostering customer loyalty. Across industries and sectors, firms seek to distinguish themselves and retain customers by excellence in service performance. Yet service management and improvement present particular challenges to managers. Unlike goods, which offer tangible measures of quality such as durability and number of defects, service performance is intangible and heterogeneous: every customer's service experience varies. Further, one cannot separate the production and consumption of service quality: a service is "produced" by the firm and "consumed" by the customer at each encounter.

Services marketing emerged as a significant subdiscipline of marketing in the mid-1980s, and in the two decades since, service quality has garnered a significant amount of research attention. Today, a substantial body of research offers a general consensus on how firms can understand, measure, and improve service quality.

What Is Service Quality?

Customers evaluate service quality by comparing what they expect with how a service provider actually performs. Thus, service quality can be defined as the difference between customers' expectations of service and their perceptions of actual service performance. Research shows that customers assess service quality along five dimensions:

- *Assurance:* Employees' knowledge and courtesy and their ability to inspire trust and confidence
- *Empathy:* The caring, individualized attention a firm provides its customers
- *Reliability:* A firm's ability to perform the promised service dependably and accurately

Responsiveness: Employees' willingness to help customers and provide prompt service

Tangibles: A firm's physical facilities, equipment, personnel, and communication materials

Among the five dimensions, reliability consistently emerges as most critical to customers and tangibles as least critical.

Measuring Service Quality

SERVQUAL is the dominant approach to quantitatively assessing service quality. Using a survey approach, SERVQUAL elicits ratings of customers' expectations and perceptions on each of the five dimensions (as well as their associated attributes). For example, to gauge customer expectations/perceptions regarding the reliability of a telephone company, respondents are asked to rate their disagreement/agreement (on a 1–7 scale) with pairs of statements such as the following:

Expectation: When excellent telephone companies promise to do something by a certain time, they will do so.

Perception: When XYZ promises to do something by a certain time, it does so.

The difference between the two ratings is the firm's service quality "score" for a particular attribute. These difference scores can be used to assess and improve service quality in a variety of ways, including tracking changes in ratings on individual dimensions over time, assessing firm internal service quality, and identifying customer segments that differ significantly in their assessments.

SERVQUAL was first developed in the 1980s; two decades of use, assessment, and refinement have shown it to be a robust measure of perceived service quality. On several points, however, researchers and practitioners continue to debate the merits of the SERVQUAL approach. For example, is it necessary to measure expectations? Are difference scores the most appropriate measure of service quality? Are the five dimensions generalizeable across contexts and cultures?

the idea is to have a "Client Satisfaction survey std"

→ Annual → survey → 1 manager a couple of days using SERVQUAL adapted to WL.

Improving Service Quality

Service quality improvement can be described as "closing the gap" between customers' expectations and perceptions of service. Research has identified four "company gaps" that underlie the overall shortfall in customer expectations/perceptions:

Gap 1: Not Knowing What Customers Expect   Many factors can obscure a firm's understanding of customer expectations, among them inadequate market research, a lack of communication from frontline employees to management, and inadequate attention to service recovery. To address this shortfall, companies need to establish "listening systems" that capture, organize, and disseminate service quality information to support decision making. Such systems might include transactional surveys, mystery shopping, focus group interviews, customer surveys, and service reviews. (Client Service quality meetings)

Gap 2: Not Selecting the Right Service Designs and Standards   Too often, firms use designs and standards that correspond to company concerns such as productivity or efficiency rather than to customer expectations and priorities. How can firms establish customer-driven service designs and standards? A multi-step process includes identifying a service encounter sequence, translating customer expectations into behaviors and actions for that sequence, developing standards for selected behaviors and actions, and developing measures, targets, and feedback mechanisms for employees. In addition, strategies such as quality function deployment or service "blueprinting" (which depicts all the players and processes in a service encounter) may help firms link customer expectations and requirements with new and existing service process designs.

Gap 3: Not Delivering to Service Standards   Even when customer-driven standards are in place, they must be enforced by a firm's employees, systems, and technology. Thus, gap 3—not delivering to service standards—addresses human resource issues such as recruitment, training, feedback, job design, motivation, and organizational structure. In addition, companies that deliver services through intermediaries such as retailers, franchisees, and brokers must ensure that such agents deliver to the company service standards.

Gap 4: Not Matching Performance to Promises   Advertising, sales force, and other communications set the standard against which customers assess a company's service quality. Ensuring that all the company's external messages are aligned with what the company delivers is more difficult in services because what is delivered critically depends on employees' interactions with customers. Customers' experiences during those interactions must be consistent with the messages the company sends through advertising, public relations, the Internet, and other channels.

Returns on Service Quality: Customer Loyalty and Profitability

There is ample evidence that favorable service quality perceptions affect customer intentions to behave in positive ways—praising the firm, preferring the company over others, increasing the volume of purchases, or agreeably paying a price premium. A growing body of evidence also shows that service quality positively impacts profits via its effects on obtaining new, and retaining existing, customers.

In terms of obtaining new customers, research shows that service quality positively impacts market share, firm reputation, and the ability to command a price premium. Considerable research also shows linkages between service quality, customer retention, and profits through reduced costs, increased purchases, the ability to command price premiums, and increased positive word-of-mouth communication.

Electronic Service Quality

The Internet raises new questions about how to understand, measure, and improve service quality: emerging research finds significant differences between the online and offline contexts. For example, personal service (the empathy dimension of SERVQUAL) is not critical in online service transactions. Purchasing online appears to be a very goal-directed behavior: customers are interested in efficient transactions. Not surprisingly, fulfillment emerges as a critical dimension in electronic service quality. Although several scales have emerged to capture customer assessment of electronic service quality, none fully explain the antecedents, composition, and consequences of electronic service quality.

Tools for Managers and Researchers

Four appendices in this monograph will be useful to researchers and managers. The first describes the process through which SERVQUAL was developed and refined by Parasuraman, Zeithaml, and Berry under the sponsorship of the Marketing Science Institute and its sponsors. The second appendix provides directions, expectations statements, and perceptions statements for the SERVQUAL instrument. The third describes a multi-sector study (sponsored by MSI) to expand SERVQUAL by incorporating two different levels of expectations (minimum and desired) into service-quality measurement, and to test two alternative survey formats. The final appendix presents the two survey formats.

Introduction

The proliferation of look-alike products in many sectors, coupled with escalating competition and more demanding customers, have made service excellence one of the key marketing tools for achieving competitive differentiation and fostering customer loyalty. Service quality continues to occupy center stage in the marketing arena even as a growing number of company-customer exchanges through traditional channels are replaced by Internet-based transactions and e-commerce.

Scholarly research on service quality has paralleled practitioner interest in understanding and leveraging superior service delivery. Much of this research has occurred within the past two decades. As of the early 1980s only a handful of writings had discussed the nature of service quality (Grönroos 1982; Lehtinen and Lehtinen 1982; Lewis and Booms 1983; Sasser, Olsen, and Wyckoff 1978). However, with the emergence of services marketing as a significant subdiscipline of marketing in the mid-1980s, service quality and its measurement have occupied an increasingly prominent place in the published literature (Fisk, Brown, and Bitner 1993). Indeed, service quality is one of the most researched topics in the services field.

In the chapters that follow we summarize research on the definition of service quality; discuss SERVQUAL, a multiple-item scale to measure service quality; review a conceptual framework for improving service quality; examine the contribution of service quality to customer loyalty and profitability; examine the role and measurement of customer service in electronic contexts; and finally, propose a research agenda for addressing unresolved and emerging issues.

Valarie A. Zeithaml
A. Parasuraman

Service Quality

What Is Service Quality?

Defining Service Quality

Early writing on the topic of service quality suggested that perceived service quality results from a comparison of what customers feel a service provider should offer (i.e., their expectations) with how the provider actually performs (Grönroos 1982; Lehtinen and Lehtinen 1982; Lewis and Booms 1983; Sasser, Olsen, and Wyckoff 1978). For instance, according to Lewis and Booms (1983), "Service quality is a measure of how well the service level delivered matches customer expectations. Delivering quality service means conforming to customer expectations on a consistent basis."

The notion that service quality can be defined as the difference between a customer's expectation of performance and his or her perception of actual performance was reinforced in a multi-sector study conducted in 1985 by Parasuraman, Zeithaml, and Berry (hereafter referred to as PZB). This study involved 12 customer focus group interviews— 3 in each of four different service sectors (retail banking, credit card, stock brokerage, and appliance repair and maintenance)—to explore how customers assessed service quality. Based on common insights from the focus groups, PZB (1985) formally defined service quality as *the degree and direction of discrepancy between customers' service perceptions and expectations.*

Dimensions of Service Quality

Early conceptualizations suggested several general service aspects that customers might use to assess service quality. Sasser, Olsen, and Wyckoff (1978) proposed three dimensions of service performance, all dealing with the *process* of service delivery: levels of material, facilities, and personnel. Grönroos (1982) proposed two types of service quality: technical quality, which involves what customers actually receive from the service provider (i.e., the *outcome* of the service) and functional quality, which involves the manner in which customers receive the service (i.e., the *process* of service delivery). Lehtinen and Lehtinen (1982) discussed three kinds of service quality: physical quality, involving physical aspects associated with the service such as equipment or building; corporate quality, involving a service firm's image or reputation; and interactive quality, involving interactions between service personnel and customers, as well as among customers.

A consistent theme emerging in this research is that customers use more than just the service outcome or "core" in assessing service quality. Customer assessments are also influenced by the service process and the "peripherals" associated with the service. The customer focus group research conducted by PZB (1985) confirmed that both outcome and process dimensions influence customers' evaluation of service quality. In addition, focus group response patterns revealed 10 general evaluative criteria that customers might use, regardless of service sector. These criteria were consistent with previously outlined service constructs, yet constituted a more comprehensive set of dimensions. They are defined as follows (with illustrative questions):

1. *Tangibles:* Appearance of physical facilities, equipment, personnel, and communication materials. Do the tools used by the repairperson look modern? Does the equipment seem modern and effective? Are personnel dressed neatly and appropriately?

2. *Reliability:* Ability to perform the promised service dependably and accurately. Does my stock broker follow my exact instructions to buy or to sell? Is the service performed right the first time? At the right time?

3. *Responsiveness:* Willingness to help customers and provide prompt service. Is my banker willing to answer my questions? When there is a problem with my bank statement, does the bank resolve the problem quickly? How quickly are my calls returned and my questions answered?

4. *Competence:* Possession of the required skills and knowledge to perform the service. When I call my credit card company, is the person at

the other end able to answer my questions? Does the repairperson appear to know what he or she is doing?

5. *Courtesy:* Politeness, respect, consideration, and friendliness of contact personnel. Does the bank teller have a pleasant demeanor? Does my broker refrain from acting busy or being rude when I ask questions?

6. *Credibility:* Trustworthiness, believability, and honesty. Does my bank have a good reputation? Does the repair firm guarantee its services?

7. *Security:* Freedom from danger, risk, or doubt. Is it safe for me to use the bank's automatic teller machines? How confidential are my financial transactions with the company?

8. *Access:* Approachability and ease of contact. How easy is it for me to get through to my broker over the telephone? Does the credit card company have a 24-hour, toll-free telephone number?

9. *Communication:* Keeping customers informed in language they can understand and listening to them. Does my broker avoid using technical jargon? Does the repair firm call when they are unable to keep a scheduled repair appointment?

10. *Understanding the customer:* Making the effort to know customers and their needs. Does someone in my bank recognize me as a regular customer? Is the credit limit set by my credit card company consistent with what I can afford (i.e., neither too high nor too low)?

After an empirical analysis to determine inter-relationships among these dimensions (PZB 1988), 3 of the original 10 remained intact: tangibles, reliability, and responsiveness. The remaining 7 clustered into 2 broader dimensions which PZB (1988) labeled assurance and empathy. Thus, the final set of five dimensions is as follows:

1. *Assurance:* Knowledge and courtesy of employees and their ability to inspire trust and confidence (combines original dimensions of competence, courtesy, credibility, and security)

2. *Empathy:* Caring, individualized attention the firm provides its customers (combines original dimensions of access, communication, and understanding the customer)

3. *Reliability:* Ability to perform the promised service dependably and accurately

4. *Responsiveness:* Willingness to help customers and provide prompt service

5. *Tangibles:* Appearance of physical facilities, equipment, personnel, and communication materials

Comparison with Product Quality

The concept of perceived quality (covering both services and products) has been broadly defined as "superiority or excellence" (Zeithaml 1988). Consistent with what has been described about service quality, perceived product quality is different from objective or actual quality; it is a higher-level abstraction rather than a specific attribute of a product, a global assessment that in some cases resembles attitude, and a judgment made within a consumer's evoked set (Zeithaml 1988, p. 3). The literature on product quality, while wide ranging and prolific, has not produced a consensus on its dimensions, although some work has attempted to do so. Bonner and Nelson (1985), for example, found that sensory signals such as rich/full flavor, natural taste, fresh taste, good aroma, and appetizing looks were relevant across 33 food product categories. Brucks, Zeithaml, and Naylor (2000) contend on the basis of both exploratory and empirical work that six abstract dimensions (ease of use, functionality, performance, durability, serviceability, and prestige) can be generalized across categories of durable goods. Garvin (1983) proposed, but did not empirically validate, eight dimensions of product quality: performance, features, reliability, conformance, durability, serviceability, aesthetics, and image.

Besides the lack of consensus regarding the dimensions that comprise product quality, researchers have also tended not to emphasize the comparison between expectations and perceptions when conceptualizing and operationalizing product quality. While customers are likely to have expectations for products just as they do for services, this point is not explicitly made or tested in existing research.

Measuring Service Quality: SERVQUAL

Having defined the concept of service quality, researchers needed to develop a sound measure of the construct. What service attributes require improvement in order to enhance quality? What degree or amount of improvement is required? How can the impact of service quality improvement efforts be assessed? Unlike goods quality, which can be measured objectively by such indicators as durability and number of defects (Crosby 1979; Garvin 1983), service quality is an abstract and elusive construct. Service quality is intangible and heterogeneous (i.e., every customer's service experience varies). Further, the production and consumption of service quality are inseparable: service is "produced" by the firm and "consumed" by the customer at the time of the service encounter (PZB 1985). In the absence of objective measures, one has to rely on survey-based measures. Given these characteristics, survey-based measures are most suited to measuring service quality. One of the first such measures was the SERVQUAL scale (PZB 1988).

SERVQUAL Development and Refinement

The original SERVQUAL scale (PZB 1988) involved a two-part survey containing 22 service attributes, grouped into the five dimensions of assurance, empathy, reliability, responsiveness, and tangibles. The 1988 survey asked customers to provide two ratings on each attribute—one reflecting their *expectations* of the level of service delivered by excellent companies in a sector and the other reflecting their *perceptions* of the service delivered by a specific company within that sector. Thus, the expectations scale measured the extent to which customers felt companies in the sector in question *should* possess a specified service attribute, and the perceptions scale measured the extent to which customers felt a given company *did* possess the attribute.

Each attribute was cast in the form of a statement with which customers were asked to express their degree of agreement or disagreement on a 7-point scale ("strongly agree" (7) at one end and "strongly disagree" (1) at the other). For example:

Expectations statement: The behavior of employees of banks should instill confidence in customers.

Corresponding perceptions statement: The behavior of employees of XYZ Bank instills confidence in customers.

Expectations statement: Banks should give customers individual attention.

Corresponding perceptions statement: XYZ Bank gives customers individual attention.

The difference between the expectation and perception ratings constituted a quantified measure of service quality.

Appendix 1 offers a detailed discussion of the construction, development, and refinement of the original SERVQUAL scale. The refined SERVQUAL instrument (including instructions to respondents) used in the five-company study (PBZ 1991b) is shown in Appendix 2. This includes a "point-allocation question" that was used to ascertain the relative importance of the five dimensions by asking respondents to allocate a total of 100 points among the dimensions. Results from this question were consistent across the five company samples in PBZ (1991b): reliability always emerged as the most critical dimension (its average allocation was 32 points) and tangibles as the least critical dimension (its average allocation was 11 points). The average allocations for responsiveness, assurance, and empathy were 23, 19, and 17 points, respectively.

SERVQUAL: Potential Uses and Applications

The SERVQUAL scale can be used by firms in the following ways:[1]

1. To determine the average gap score (between customers' perceptions and expectations) for each service attribute.

2. To assess a company's service quality along each of the five SERVQUAL dimensions.

3. To compute a company's overall *weighted* SERVQUAL score that takes into account not only the service quality gap on each dimension but also the relative importance of the dimension (as reflected by the number of points out of 100 that customers allocate to it).

4. To track customers' expectations and perceptions (on individual service attributes and/or on the SERVQUAL dimensions) over time.

5. To compare a company's SERVQUAL scores against those of competitors.

6. To identify and examine customer segments that differ significantly in their assessments of a company's service performance.

7. To assess *internal* service quality (i.e., the quality of service rendered by one department or division of a company to others within the same company).

It is important to note that SERVQUAL is not a panacea for all service-quality measurement problems, nor should it be used by companies as the sole basis for assessing service quality. Rather, it should be viewed as a component of a more comprehensive service quality information system (Berry and Parasuraman 1991). As PZB (1988) observed: "The instrument has been designed to be applicable across a broad spectrum of services. As such, it provides a basic skeleton through its expectations/perceptions format encompassing statements for each of the five service-quality dimensions. The skeleton, when necessary, can be adapted or supplemented to fit the characteristics or specific research needs of a particular organization. SERVQUAL is most valuable when it is used periodically to track service quality trends, *and when it is used in conjunction with other forms of service quality measurement*" [emphasis added] (pp. 30–31).

Studies and Applications

A series of published studies have used SERVQUAL and adaptations of it in a variety of contexts—e.g., real estate brokerages (Johnson, Dotson, and Dunlop 1988); physicians' private practice (Brown and Swartz 1989); public recreation programs (Crompton and Mackay 1989); a dental school patient clinic, business school placement center, and tire store (Carman

1990); motor carrier companies (Brensinger and Lambert 1990); an accounting firm (Bojanic 1991); discount and department stores (Finn and Lamb 1991; Teas 1993); a gas and electric utility company (Babakus and Boller 1992); hospitals (Babakus and Mangold 1992; Carman 1990); banking, pest control, dry cleaning, and fast food companies (Cronin and Taylor 1992); and higher education institutions (Boulding, Kalra, Staelin, and Zeithaml 1993; Ford, Joseph, and Joseph 1993).

SERVQUAL has been productively used in multiple contexts, cultures, and countries for measuring service quality in commercial as well as public sector organizations. The nature of and findings from virtually all of these applications are unpublished and/or proprietary. However, based on the authors' knowledge (and with appropriate protection of confidentiality), two applications are briefly described below.

Consumer-Service Context   A large Australian bank used SERVQUAL to measure its quality of service as evaluated by several segments of individual customers. The bank analyzed the data to assess service quality deficiencies on individual attributes and on the five SERVQUAL dimensions as well as to compute weighted gap scores. The bank also benchmarked its SERVQUAL scores against those of two similar banks in the United States that had participated in studies conducted by PBZ. While some differences between the results for the Australian and U.S. banks were found on specific service attributes, there were striking similarities in the overall pattern of results. For instance, the relative importance of the five dimensions (as measured by the point-allocation question) was as follows:

	Australian Bank	U.S. Bank 1	U.S. Bank 2
Tangibles	13*	10	11
Reliability	28	31	32
Responsiveness	22	22	22
Assurance	19	20	19
Empathy	18	17	16

*Number of points allocated out of 100.

The Australian bank set up a measurement system to track service quality at regular intervals and to assess the impact of service improvement efforts.

Industrial-Product Context   The Ceramic Products Division of Corning, Inc., a large manufacturing company in the United States, developed a systematic process for monitoring and improving its service quality as perceived by customer organizations to which it supplied its manufactured products. The SERVQUAL approach was an integral component of this process (Farley, Daniels, and Pearl 1990).

Corning's Ceramic Products Division began its service-improvement process by focusing on its largest client, a multinational company. The division modified the SERVQUAL instrument for assessing its service quality and that of its primary competitors as perceived by multiple levels within this company. Individuals at various functional levels completed the survey. Analysis of the responses revealed seven service attributes on which Corning's performance was weakest. Corning further condensed this short list of attributes to four "vital few" attributes on which its performance was worse than that of its major competitor, then formed a corrective action team to identify and implement action plans to improve its service quality on the vital attributes.

The SERVQUAL survey was re-administered a year later to assess the impact of the corrective actions. Results indicated significant improvements in most of the targeted attributes and also identified additional areas for corrective action. The success of using SERVQUAL in this pilot application prompted Corning to make this process an ongoing activity in the Ceramics Product Division and to expand its implementation to other divisions and customer groups.

Criticisms of SERVQUAL

The SERVQUAL scale has been the subject of criticism and debate in many published studies.[2] The major questions can be summarized as follows:

Is It Necessary to Measure Expectations?   Studies have shown consistently that scores on the perceptions-only component of SERVQUAL are able to explain significantly more variance in customers' overall evaluations of an organization's service quality (measured on a single-item, overall-perceptions rating scale) than are the perception-expectation difference scores. Thus, from a strictly predictive-validity standpoint, measuring expectations is not warranted. Moreover, measuring expectations increases survey length. However, SERVQUAL's developers have argued that measuring expectations has diagnostic value (i.e., it generates information that will pinpoint shortfalls in service quality) and that basing service-improvement decisions solely on perceptions data might lead to suboptimal or erroneous resource allocations (PZB 1994a). Additionally, from a practitioner's standpoint, an equally important purpose is to pinpoint service quality shortfalls and take appropriate corrective action. From this *diagnostic-value* perspective, it is prudent to measure perceptions against expectations. For a fuller discussion of this question, and a multi-sector study, see Appendix 3.

How Should the Expectations Construct Be Operationalized? Although the definition of service quality as the gap between customers' expectations and perceptions is conceptually simple, the operationalization of this definition has been controversial because of the multiple ways the term "expectation" can be and has been interpreted. While service quality researchers have generally viewed expectations as normative standards (i.e., customers' beliefs about what a service provider *should* offer), researchers working in the area of customer satisfaction/dissatisfaction have typically considered expectations to be predictive standards (i.e., what customers feel a service provider *will* offer). However, both "should" and "will" expectations have been used in measuring service quality (Boulding, Kalra, Staelin, and Zeithaml 1993). Furthermore, other types of expectations (e.g., "ideal," "deserved") have been proposed and defended as appropriate comparison standards (for a comprehensive review, see Woodruff, Clemons, Schumann, Gardial, and Burns 1991).

In an attempt to address these unresolved issues in the area of customer expectations, ZBP (1993) developed a conceptual model of expectations by combining insights from past research with findings from a multi-sector study aimed at understanding the nature and determinants of customers' service expectations.

ZBP (1993) developed a conceptual model of expectations that suggested that customers use two different comparison standards in assessing service quality: desired service—*the level of service representing a blend of what customers believe "can be" and "should be" provided*; and adequate service—*the minimum level of service customers are willing to accept*. Separating these two levels is a "zone of tolerance" that represents the range of service performance a customer would consider satisfactory.

Although SERVQUAL's original expectations component measures normative expectations (i.e., the *desired* service construct) it did not capture the *adequate* service construct. Therefore, in a multi-sector study (PZB 1994b), SERVQUAL was augmented and refined to capture not only the discrepancy between perceived service and desired service, which was labeled as *measure of service superiority* (or MSS), but also the discrepancy between perceived service and adequate service–labeled as *measure of service adequacy* (or MSA). See Appendix 3 for details.

The results of the study (PBZ1991b) provide support for the meaningfulness of using the zone of tolerance (bounded by the desired and adequate service expectations) as a yardstick against which to compare perceived service performance. Operationalizing customer expectations as a zone or range of service levels is not only feasible empirically but also valuable from a diagnostic standpoint. Using the zone of tolerance as a comparison standard in evaluating service performance can help companies in understanding how well they are meeting at least customers' minimum requirements, and how much improvement is needed before they achieve the status of service superiority.

Is It Appropriate to Operationalize Service Quality as a Difference Score?
Operationalizing a construct as a difference between two other constructs may be questioned for psychometric reasons, especially if the difference scores are to be used in multivariate analyses (for a review of concerns, see Peter, Churchill, and Brown 1993). SERVQUAL's difference-score formulation has been questioned on this basis (Babakus and Boller 1992; Brown, Churchill, and Peter 1993). Some critics have suggested that direct (i.e., non-difference score) measures of the perception-expectation gap will be psychometrically superior (e.g., Carman 1990; Peter, Churchill, and Brown 1993). However, empirical comparisons of SERVQUAL and direct measures of service quality have not established conclusively that the direct measures are superior (PBZ 1993).

To assess the relative merits and demerits of the difference-score and direct operationalizations of the service quality gap measures (i.e., MSS and MSA), two measurement formats were tested in the (PZB 1994a) study (see appendices 3 and 4). Further the study examined the reliability, validity, and diagnostic value of the direct and difference-score measures. Both the direct and difference-score measures of service quality fared well.

From a practical or diagnostic-value standpoint, the difference-score measures had another advantage—by virtue of its generating separate ratings of the adequate-service, desired-service, and perception levels, this format is capable of *pinpointing* the position of the zone of tolerance and the perceived service level relative to the zone. In contrast, the direct measures indicate whether the perceived service level is above, below, or within the tolerance zone. They cannot identify the tolerance zone's position on a continuum of expectation levels; nor can they pinpoint the perceived service level relative to the zone.

In summary, the difference-score operationalization of service quality appears to have psychometric properties that are as sound as those of the direct-measure operationalization. Moreover, difference-score measures yield richer diagnostics than direct-score measures. Thus, operationalizing service quality as difference scores seems appropriate.

Does SERVQUAL Have Five Distinct Dimensions That Transcend Different Contexts? Replication studies incorporating SERVQUAL have not been able to reproduce as "clean" a five-dimensional factor structure as was obtained in the original study (PZB 1988). For instance, in an article comparing and synthesizing results from several replication studies, PBZ (1991a) point out that the number of final SERVQUAL dimensions vary from two (Babakus and Boller 1992) to five (Brensinger and Lambert 1990) to eight (Carman 1990). PBZ (1991b) offer several explanations for these differences: "Respondents may indeed consider the SERVQUAL dimensions to be conceptually distinct; however, if their evaluations of a specific company on individual scale items are similar *across* dimensions, fewer than five dimensions will result as in the Babakus and Boller (1992) study. Alternatively, if their evaluations of a company on scale items *within* a dimension are sufficiently distinct, more than five dimensions will result as in Carman's (1990) study. In other words, differences in the number of empirically derived factors across replications may be primarily due to across-dimension similarities and/or within-dimension differences in customers' evaluations of a *specific* company involved in each setting. At a *general* level, the five-dimensional structure of SERVQUAL may still serve as a meaningful framework for summarizing the criteria customers use in assessing service quality" (p. 440). Nevertheless, the dimensionality of SERVQUAL continues to be debated (e.g., Cronin and Taylor 1992; PZB 1994a) and, as such, is an issue warranting further research.

Cultural Differences

The development of service quality dimensions was based on research conducted across multiple contexts within the United States. As a general rule, reliability has been found to be the most important dimension of service quality in the United States, with responsiveness typically the second most important. One question that researchers have begun to investigate is whether the dimensions and the relative importance of the dimensions are the same across cultures. To study this question, researchers have used Hofstede's well-established cultural dimensions, which include power distance, individualism, collectivism, masculinity, uncertainty avoidance, and long-term orientation (Hofstede 1991).

Furrer, Liu, and Sudharshan (2000) found strong differences in the importance of the five service quality dimensions across clusters of customers defined by Hofstede's cultural dimensions. They identified five clusters, which they called followers, balance seekers, self-confidents, sensory seekers, and functional analyzers, and found differences across clusters in the importance of the five service quality dimensions. For example, self-confidents and functional analyzers rated reliability and responsiveness as most important; followers and sensory seekers rate these two dimensions as relatively unimportant. The tangibles dimension shows the widest variation, with sensory seekers rating it most important and functional analyzers rating it least important.

Winsted (1997), in a study investigating how consumers in the United States and Japan evaluate service encounters, identified significant cross-cultural differences in behavioral-based service encounter dimensions. In the United States, the dimensions included civility, personalization, remembering, conversation, congeniality, delivery, and authenticity, while in Japan they were civility, personalization, conversation, concern, and formality. Mattila (1999) conducted a study to understand the trade-offs that Western and Asian customers are willing to make between personalized service and pleasant physical environment in luxury hotels. Findings suggested that customers with a Western cultural background are more likely to rely on tangible cues from the environment than Asians. Donthu and Yoo (1998) researched the effect of customers' cultural orientation on their service quality expectations using Hofstede's cultural dimensions and the five service quality dimensions. Results showed that all consumers had high overall service quality expectations but differences occurred on the dimensions where expectations were highest. Consumers low on power distance expected responsive and reliable service, while individualistic consumers expected empathy and assurance.

Improving Service Quality

The Gaps Model of Service Quality

Closing the customer gap—delivering quality service—is a complex undertaking involving many different organizational and employee skills and tasks (ZBP 1988). Executives of services organizations have long been confused about how to approach this complicated topic in an organized manner. PZB (1985) developed one approach to viewing the delivery of service quality in a structured and integrated way: the "gaps model" of service quality. The gaps model positions the key concepts, strategies, and decisions in delivering quality service in a manner that begins with the customer and builds the organization's tasks around what is needed to close the gap between customer expectations and perceptions (see figure).

The figure shows that the central focus (top half) of the gaps model is the customer gap. To close this all-important customer gap, the model suggests that four other gaps—the provider gaps—need to be closed. These are the underlying causes of the customer gap:

Gap 1: Not Knowing What Customers Expect   Provider gap 1 is the difference between customer expectations of service and company, particularly management, understanding of those expectations. There are many reasons why managers may not be aware of what customers expect: they may not interact directly with customers, they may be unwilling to ask about expectations, or they may be unprepared to address them. Further, because there are few clearly defined and tangible cues for services, this gap may be considerably larger than it is in firms that produce tangible goods (Grönroos 1982; Webster 1992). When people with the authority and responsibility for setting priorities do not fully understand customers' service expectations, they may trigger a chain of bad decisions and sub-optimal resource allocations that result in perceptions of poor service quality.

Figure 1 ■ THE GAPS MODEL OF SERVICE QUALITY

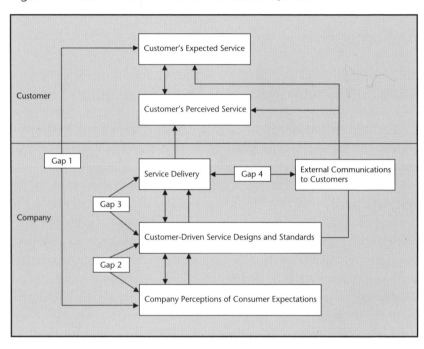

A number of factors have been shown to be responsible for provider gap 1. First, because marketing research is a key vehicle for understanding consumer expectations and perceptions of services, the size of gap 1 depends greatly on the amount of marketing research conducted (ZBP 1988). Evidence indicates that service firms lag behind goods firms in their use of marketing research and in other facets of customer orientation. A second factor is lack of upward communication. Frontline employees often know a great deal about customers (Schneider and Bowen 1985), but management may not be in contact with frontline employees and may not understand what they know. A third factor is a lack of company strategies to retain customers and strengthen relationships with them (Berry 1983; Gwinner, Gremler, and Bitner 1998). A fourth factor is inadequate attention to service recovery—understanding why people complain and what they expect when they complain, and how to develop effective strategies for dealing with inevitable service failures (Tax and Brown 1998).

Gap 2: The Wrong Service Quality Designs and Standards   A recurring challenge in service companies is the difficulty of translating customers' expectations into service quality specifications. Thus, provider gap 2 reflects the difference between company understanding of customer expectations and development of *customer-driven service designs and standards*. Customer-driven standards differ from the conventional performance standards that most services companies establish in that they are based on pivotal customer requirements that are visible to and measured by customers (Zeithaml and Bitner 2003). They are operations standards set to correspond to customer expectations and priorities rather than to company concerns such as productivity or efficiency. Standards signal to contact personnel what management priorities are and which types of performance really count. When service standards are absent or when the standards in place do not reflect customers' expectations, quality of service as perceived by customers is likely to suffer (Levitt 1976).

Because services are intangible, they are difficult to describe and communicate, a particularly difficult problem when new services are being developed. When all people involved (managers, frontline employees, and behind-the-scenes support staff) are not working with the same concepts of the new service, based on customer needs and expectations, service design will likely be poor (Shostack 1992). For a service that already exists, any attempt to improve it will also suffer if people do not have the same vision of the service, which results in oversimplification, incompleteness, subjectivity, and bias (Shostack 1992).

Gap 3: Not Delivering to Service Standards   Provider gap 3 is the discrepancy between development of customer-driven service standards and actual service performance by company employees. Even when guidelines exist for performing services well and treating customers correctly, high-quality service performance is not a certainty. Standards must be backed by appropriate resources (people, systems, and technology) and also must be enforced to be effective—that is, employees must be measured and compensated on the basis of performance along those standards (ZBP 1988). Thus, even when standards accurately reflect customers' expectations, if the company fails to provide support for them—if it does not facilitate, encourage, and require their achievement—standards do no good. When the level of service-delivery performance falls short of the standards, it misses what customers expect as well. Narrowing gap 3 by ensuring that all the resources needed to achieve the standards are in place reduces the customer gap.

Research and company experience have identified many of the critical inhibitors to closing gap 3 (Schneider and Bowen 1993). These include employees who do not clearly understand their role (Katz and Kahn 1978; Walker, Churchill, and Ford 1977), employees who feel caught in the middle between customers and company management (Rizzo, House, and Lirtzman 1970), the wrong employees (Bettencourt and Gwinner 1996; Schneider and Schechter 1991), inadequate technology, inappropriate compensation, and recognition (Ouchi and McGuire 1975), and lack of empowerment and teamwork (Bowen and Lawler 1992). These factors all relate to the company's human resource function, involving internal practices such as recruitment, training, feedback, job design, motivation, and organizational structure.

Other problems involve the challenge of delivering service through intermediaries such as retailers, franchisees, agents, and brokers (Bongiorno 1993). Most service (and many manufacturing) companies face formidable problems in attaining service excellence and consistency in the presence of intermediaries who represent them, interact with their customers, and yet are not under their direct control (Serwer 1995). Even if contact employees and intermediaries are 100% consistent in their service delivery, the customer can introduce heterogeneity in service delivery (Grove and Fisk 1997). If customers do not perform their roles appropriately—if, for example, they fail to provide all the information necessary to the provider or neglect to read and follow instructions—service quality is jeopardized (Kelley, Skinner, and Donnelly 1992).

Gap 4: Not Matching Performance to Promise   Provider gap 4 is the difference between service delivery and the service provider's external communications. Promises made by a service company through its media advertising, sales force, and other communications may raise customer expectations and serve as the standard against which customers assess service quality (ZBP 1988). The discrepancy between actual and promised service therefore has an adverse effect on the customer gap. Broken promises can occur for many reasons: over-promising in advertising or personal selling, inadequate coordination between operations and marketing, and differences in policies and procedures across service outlets (George and Berry 1981). In addition to unduly elevating expectations through exaggerated claims, there are other, less obvious ways in which external communications influence customers' service quality assessments. Service companies frequently fail to capitalize on opportunities to educate customers to use services appropriately (Legg and Baker 1991). They also frequently fail to manage customer expectations of what they will receive in service transactions and relationships.

Closing the Gaps

What strategies can be used to close these gaps and improve service quality? These are described below, organized according to the service quality gap they address.

Determining What Customers Expect   To close gap 1, companies must use multiple research approaches among different customer groups to ensure that they are hearing what customers expect. Berry and Parasuraman (1997) argue that companies need to establish ongoing listening systems to capture, organize, and disseminate service quality information to support decision making. These include transactional surveys; mystery shopping; focus group interviews; new, declining, and lost customer surveys; and service reviews.

A good listening system could incorporate approaches to address all possible reasons for not understanding what customers expect. It could, for example, continuously solicit employee input that would allow for upward communication, identify market segments, encourage management-customer interaction, focus on understanding customer relationships, and identify the failures that require service recovery.

Developing Customer-Driven Standards and Designs   To close gap 2, service providers must match new-service innovations and actual service process designs to customer expectations. Research shows that adaptations of the new-product design process can make service offerings more explicit and avoid failures (Zeithaml and Bitner 2003). Service "blueprinting" is a particularly useful technique in the new-service development process (Kingman-Brundage 1991; Shostack 1992). The purpose of a blueprint is to make a complex and intangible service concrete through its visual depiction of all of the steps, actors, processes, and physical evidence of the service (Bitner 1993). The key feature of service blueprints is their focus on the customer: the customer's experience is documented before any of the internal processes are determined. Quality function deployment (QFD) is another tool for linking customer requirements to internal elements of service design (Fitzsimmons and Fitzsimmons 1997; Harvey 1998). The other key strategy essential for closing gap 2 is establishing customer-driven service standards, which can either take the form of operational (hard) or perceptual (soft) standards. Zeithaml and Bitner (2003) recommend a nine-step process for developing these standards: (1) identify existing or desired service encounter sequence, (2) translate customer expectations into behaviors and actions for each service encounter, (3) select behaviors and actions for standards, (4) decide whether hard or soft standards are appropriate, (5) develop feedback mechanisms for measurement to standards, (6) establish measures and target levels, (7) track measures against standards, (8) provide feedback about performance to employees, and (9) periodically update target levels and measures. Successful development of customer-driven standards is discussed in Levitt (1976), Camp (1989), Ehrenfeld (1991), and Carroll (1992). One of the areas that seems most in need of customer-defined standards is waiting for service (Taylor 1994).

Improving Service Performance   Because most services are delivered by people to people in real time, closing the service performance gap is heavily dependent on human resource strategies. Research shows that employee and customer satisfaction are positively correlated (Schlesinger and Heskett 1991), as are climate for service, climate for employee well-being, and customer perceptions of service quality (Schneider and Bowen 1993). Research shows that employee responses—particularly with respect to service delivery system failures and customer needs and requests—and unsolicited employee actions to help customers are largely responsible for customers' evaluations of service encounters (Bitner, Booms, and Tetreault 1990). Considerable research has been conducted on strategies for integrating appropriate human resource practices into service firms. Among these strategies are: addressing role ambiguity and role conflict (Hartline and Ferrell 1996; Singh, Goolsby, and Rhoads 1994), optimizing employee-technology-job fit (Berry and Parasuraman 1991; Fisher 1998; Schneider and Schechter 1991), training (Normann 1984), developing appropriate evaluation and compensation systems (Chung and Schneider 1999), supervisor communication practices (Johlke and Duhan 2000), empowerment (Bowen and Lawler 1992; Chebat and Kollias 2000), teamwork (Dickson 1994), organizational citizenship (Kelley and Hoffman 1997), organizational learning (Hays and Hill 2001), and developing a service culture (Schneider and Bowen 1995). These strategies are aimed at allowing employees to be effective in satisfying customers as well as efficient and productive in their jobs. Strategies designed to manage the customer in closing gap 3 have also been proposed and studied. Zeithaml and Bitner (2003) delineated three approaches: defining customers' roles in service delivery (Winslow 1992), managing the customer mix (Martin and Pranter 1989), and recruiting, educating, and rewarding customers (e.g., Bowen 1986; Goodwin 1988).

Managing Service Promises One of the most important strategies in managing service promises involves aligning all of the company's individual external and internal messages so that integrated marketing communication (IMC) is achieved. This is more difficult to attain in services than in goods because many of the most important communication exchanges are between employees and customers; therefore the messages employees give to customers must be consistent with the messages the company sends through advertising, public relations, the Internet, and other channels (Bell and Leavitt 1998). Among the issues associated with achieving IMC are managing service promises (George and Berry 1981; Legg and Baker 1991), managing internal marketing communications, improving customer education, and managing customer expectations (Clemmer and Schneider 1993; PBZ 1991a). Explicit service promises, such as guarantees and warranties, have been found to be effective ways to increase customer perceptions of service reliability (Andaleeb 1998).

Return on Service Quality: Customer Loyalty and Profitability

Behavioral Consequences of Service Quality

Published research offers evidence that positive service quality perceptions affect customer intentions to behave in positive ways. However, most of the early research operationalized behavioral intentions in a uni-dimensional way rather than delineated specific types of behavioral intentions. Woodside, Frey, and Daly (1989), for example, found a significant association between overall patient satisfaction and intent to choose a hospital again. Cronin and Taylor (1992), using a single-item purchase-intention scale, found a positive correlation with service quality and purchase intention.

Several academic studies did examine the association between service quality and more specific behavioral intentions. In a series of studies (see PBZ 1991b; PZB 1988, 1994b) researchers found a positive and significant relationship between customers' perceptions of service quality and their willingness to recommend the company. Boulding and colleagues (1993) found a positive correlation between service quality and a two-item measure of repurchase intentions and willingness to recommend. In a second study involving university students, they found strong links between service quality and other behavioral intentions that are of strategic importance to a university, including willingness to say positive things about the school, planning to contribute money to the class pledge upon graduation, and planning to recommend the school to employers as a place from which to recruit (Boulding, Staelin, Kalra, and Zeithaml 1992).

ZBP (1996) empirically examined the quality-intentions link using a behavioral intentions battery with four dimensions—loyalty, propensity to switch, willingness to pay more, and external response (complaining to entities other than the provider itself) to service problems—comprising 14 specific behavioral intentions likely to result from perceived service quality. The dimensions and the battery were significantly correlated with customer perceptions of service quality.

Individual companies have also monitored the impact of service quality on selected behavioral intentions. Toyota found that intent to repurchase a Toyota automobile increased from 37% to 45% with a positive sales experience, from 37% to 79% with a positive service experience, and from 37% to 91% with both positive sales and service experiences (McLaughlin 1993). A similar study by Gale (1992) quantitatively assessed the relationship between level of service quality and willingness to purchase at AT&T. Of AT&T's customers who rated the company's overall quality as excellent, over 90% expressed willingness to purchase from AT&T again. For customers rating the service as good, fair, or poor, the percentages decreased to 60%, 17%, and 0%, respectively. According to these data, willingness to repurchase increased at a steeper rate (i.e., by 43%) as the service-quality rating improved from fair to good than when it went from poor to fair (17%) or from good to excellent (30%). These results suggest that the impact of service quality on willingness to repurchase is most pronounced at an intermediate level of service quality.

Service Quality and Profitability

In the 1980s, expenditures on quality were not explicitly linked to profit implications (Aaker and Jacobson 1994), largely because the evidence was not readily available. The cost of, and cost savings due to, service quality were more frequently considered because evidence linking those financial variables to service quality was more accessible. The relationship between service and profits took time to verify, partly due to the unfounded expectation that the connection was simple and direct. Despite this expectation, investments in service quality do not track directly to profits.

First, like advertising benefits, service quality benefits are rarely experienced in the short term and instead accumulate over time, making them less amenable to traditional research approaches that tend to measure short-term impact. Second, since many other variables (such as pricing, distribution, competition, and advertising) influence company profits, it can be difficult to isolate the individual contribution of service. Third, mere expenditures on service are not what lead to profits; instead spending on the right variables and proper execution are responsible.

Despite this, at the aggregate level a growing body of evidence is emerging about the relationship between service quality and profitability. This research stream began in the late 1990s when firms sought documentation that their investments in service quality, and in TQM in general, were paying off. Because individual firms found it difficult to substantiate the impact of their investments, they turned for insight to early studies conducted by management consulting firms that explored effects across a broad sample of firms. The news was not encouraging. McKinsey and Company found that nearly two-thirds of quality programs examined had stalled or fallen short of delivering real improvements (Matthews and Katel 1992). In other studies, A. T. Kearney found that 80% of British firms reported no significant impact as a result of TQM, and Arthur D. Little claimed that almost two-thirds of 500 U.S. companies saw "zero competitive gain" from TQM (*The Economist* 1992).

Partially in response, in 1991, the U.S. General Accounting Office undertook a study of 22 companies who were finalists or winners of the Malcolm Baldrige National Quality Award in 1988 and 1989. While not a rigorous analytical study that measured common variables across companies, the GAO found that these elite quality firms had benefited in terms of market share, sales per employee, return on sales, and return on assets. The GAO found that 34 of 40 financial variables measured in 1988 or 1989 showed positive performance improvements, while only 6 measurements were negative or neutral (U.S. General Accounting Office 1991).

More rigorous academic studies soon followed, documenting both negative and positive relationships. Studies showing negative or no effects were typically not focused solely on service quality but examined TQM in general. Easton (1993), for example, showed that departmental self-interest and turf battles hampered or resulted in ineffective TQM programs in both product and service companies. Bounds, York, Adams, and Ranney (1994) and Reger, Gustafson, Demarie, and Mulland (1994) identified implementation problems that interfered with quality's impact on business performance. Sterman, Repenning, and Kofman (1997) found that a variety of quality strategies failed to deliver anticipated business performance improvements in many companies. Ittner and Larcker (1996) found that only 29% of executive respondents could link quality to accounting returns such as return on assets, and only 12% could link their TQM initiatives to stock price returns or the creation of economic value for shareholders.

Evidence from research also uncovered positive associations. Rust, Subramanian, and Wells (1992) documented the favorable financial impact of complaint recovery systems. Nelson, Rust, Zahorik, Rose, Batalden, and Siemanski (1992) found a significant and positive relationship between patient satisfaction and hospital profitability. In that study, specific dimensions of hospital service quality, such as billing and discharge processes, explained 17%–27% of the variance in financial measures such as hospital earnings, net revenues, and return on assets. Extending the definition of financial performance to include stock returns, Aaker and Jacobson (1994) found a significant positive relationship between stock return and changes in quality perceptions while controlling for the effects of advertising expenditures, salience, and ROI. In their study, the explanatory power of the quality measure was comparable to that of ROI, which was viewed as strong corroboration of the connection between perceived quality and business performance.

Indications from companies large enough to have multiple outlets also suggested a positive quality-profitability relationship. For example, the Hospital Corporation of America found a strong link between perceived quality of patient care and profitability across its many hospitals (Koska 1990). The Ford Motor Company also demonstrated that dealers with high service quality scores have higher-than-normal profit, return on investment, and profit per new vehicle sold (Ford Motor Company 1990).

Ittner and Larcker (1996) correlated the 1994 American Customer Satisfaction Index results of 130 publicly traded firms with available accounting and stock price data and documented a positive correlation between customer variables (satisfaction, repurchase intention, perceived quality, perceived value, and loyalty) with financial measures (return on assets, market-to-book ratio, and price-earnings ratio). Quality improvement has also been linked in other studies to stock price shifts (Aaker and

Jacobson 1994), the market value of the firm (Hendricks and Singhal 1997), and overall corporate performance (Easton and Jarrell 1998).

One stream of research, based largely in the operations and management literatures, has investigated the impact of service programs and managerial approaches within an organization on dependent measures, including profitability measures. For example, Fitzgerald and Erdmann (1992) estimated the impact of continuous improvement on profits in 280 automotive suppliers and found a 17% increase in profits over a two- to three-year period. Mann and Kehoe (1994) revealed that delegated teams were particularly effective at improving people and that statistical process control was most effective in improving processes in TQM programs. Ittner and Larcker (1997) explored the cross-sectional association between process management techniques and profit measures (return on sales and return on assets) and found that long-term partnerships with suppliers and customers are associated with higher performance. Furthermore, they found that other techniques (e.g., statistical process control, process capability studies, and cycle time analysis) vary by industry and are not universally related to the performance measures. A marketing study in this stream was conducted by Hauser, Simester, and Werner-felt (1994) who demonstrated analytically the financial implications of using customer satisfaction in employee incentive systems.

Rust, Zahorik, and Keiningham (1995) provided the most comprehensive framework for examining the impact of service quality improvements on profits. Called the return on quality (ROQ) approach, their framework is based on the following assumptions: (1) quality is an investment; (2) quality efforts must be financially accountable; (3) it is possible to spend too much on quality; and (4) not all quality expenditures are equally valid.

The model begins with the key drivers of service and demonstrates that the behavioral impacts of service quality lead to improved profitability and other financial outcomes. The process begins with a service improvement effort that first produces an increased level of customer satisfaction at the process or attribute level (e.g., Bolton and Drew 1991a, b; Rust, Keiningham, Clemens, and Zahorik 1998; Simester, Hauser, Wernerfelt, and Rust 1998). Increased customer satisfaction at the process or attribute level then leads to increased overall customer satisfaction or perceived service quality (Kordupleski, Rust, and Zahorik 1993; Rust, Zahorik, and Keiningham 1994, 1995). Overall satisfaction leads to behavioral impact, including repurchase or customer retention, positive word-of-mouth, and increased usage. Behavioral impact then leads to improved profitability and other financial outcomes.

By tracking impacts throughout the entire chain, the ROQ approach provides a measure of the effect of individual changes in service quality investments on overall profitability. The ROQ approach is informative because it can help distinguish among all the company strategies, processes, approaches, and tactics that can be altered and thus can be applied in companies to direct their individual strategies. Huge progress can be made in this area using the ROQ framework because it provides a solid structure for guiding practice and research.

Offensive Effects: New Customers

Fornell and Wernerfelt (1987, 1988) have defined "offensive effects" as the impact of service on obtaining new customers. Only a small set of studies exists on offensive effects, usually involving the relationship between service quality and antecedents of profitability such as market share, firm reputation, and the ability to command a price premium. Virtually all of these studies are at the aggregate level examining a cross-section of firms. Seminal studies using the PIMS (Profit Impact of Market Strategy) database uncovered significant associations among service quality, marketing variables, and profitability. Findings from these studies showed that companies offering superior service achieve higher-than-normal market share growth (Buzzell and Gale 1987) and that the mechanisms by which service quality increased profits included higher market share and premium prices (Phillips, Chang, and Buzzell 1983). In one study, Gale (1992) found that businesses in the top quintile of relative service quality on average realize an 8% higher price than their competitors.

One of the major criticisms leveled at PIMS research, and one with high relevance to linking service quality and profits, is that in PIMS perceived service quality is reported from the firm's perspective rather than the customer's perspective. Thus, while we can examine the *firm's* perception of the customer's perception of service quality and profits, we cannot examine directly the relationship between *customer* perceived quality and profits. Difficulties in data collection, specifically connecting customer data with firm data, impede these research efforts.

Kordupleski, Rust, and Zahorik (1993) conceptually delineated the path between quality and market share, claiming that satisfied customers spread positive word-of-mouth, which leads to the attraction of new customers and then to higher market share. They claim that advertising without sufficient quality to back up the communications will not increase market share. Further, they contend that there are time lags in market share effects, making the relationship between quality and market share difficult to discern in the short term.

Defensive Effects: Retaining Customers

Anecdotes about the superior financial value of existing customers over new customers are ubiquitous. Two of the most frequently cited are that it costs five times as much to obtain a new customer as to keep an existing one, and that selling costs for existing customers are much lower (on average 20%) than those for new ones (Peters 1988). Using an approach called "defensive marketing" (Fornell and Wernerfelt 1987, 1988), researchers and consulting firms have in the last ten years documented and quantified the financial impact of existing customers. These studies have found that there are numerous intervening variables that link customer retention and profits and that these variables can be isolated, calibrated, and measured within companies.

Research shows linkages between customer retention and profits through the identified intervening factors of cost, increased purchases, price premium, and word-of-mouth communication (Reichheld and Sasser 1990; Rose 1990; Dawkins and Reichheld 1990). Reichheld and Sasser (1990) demonstrate that customer loyalty can produce profit increases from 25%–85%.

Heskett, Sasser, and Schlesinger (1997) conceptualized their research as the "service-profit chain," that is, the longer that customers stay with companies, the lower the costs to serve them, the higher the volume of purchases they make, the higher the price premium they tolerate, and the greater the positive word-of-mouth communication. They provided evidence from companies such as Sears, Intuit, and Taco Bell to document these relationships (Heskett, Sasser, and Schlesinger 1997).

They found the strongest evidence of the service-profit chain at Sears. The year 1992 was the worst in the history of Sears, with a net loss of $3.9 billion on sales of $52.3 billion. From 1993–98, however, Sears transformed itself into a company built around its customers by developing a model called the 3Cs and 3Ps. The 3Cs were known as the 3 "compellings": make Sears into a "compelling place to work, shop and invest." The 3Ps were the company's three shared values—"passion for the customer, our people add value, and performance leadership." Using an ongoing process of data collection and analysis, the company created a set of Total Performance Indicators, or TPIs, measures that showed how well it was doing with customers, employees, and investors. The company developed sets of specific objectives and measures to capture the 3Cs and 3Ps, as well as goals and measures for employees. Sears management spent a great deal of time and effort in communication to and education of store-level personnel about their value and the worth of the customer. In 1998, the company declared the model successful, as shown in the following quote:

> [I]n the course of the last 12 months, employee satisfaction on the Sears TPI has risen by almost 4% and customer satisfaction by 4% . . . if our model is correct—and its predictive record is extremely good— that 4% improvement in customer satisfaction translates into more than $200 million in additional revenues in the past 12 months. (Ricci, Kirn, and Quinn 1998, p. 97)

The Impact of Selecting Profitable Customers

Most published research on the connection between service quality and profitability has reported relationships in the aggregate rather than by segments or individual customers. This is understandable, for most service quality efforts in the past treated all customers alike, usually attempting to deliver high quality to all customers. In recent years, however, both scholars and managers have identified the need to distinguish among levels or tiers of customers in providing service (Zeithaml, Rust, and Lemon 2001). Companies have successfully tiered customers by usage in industries such as airlines, hotels, and rental car companies (often undertaking frequent-flier or -buyer programs). Where heavy usage runs parallel to profitability, these programs are effective. However, many companies and industries are discovering that heavy users require both high servicing and deep discounting, leading them to be less profitable than other categories of customers.

Reichheld (1993) showed that building a high-loyalty customer base of selected customers increased profits. At MBNA, a 5% increase in retention of the right customers grew the company profits 60% by the fifth year. In later work, Reichheld (1996b) stated that companies must concentrate their efforts on that subset of customers to whom they can deliver consistently superior value. He suggests that companies isolate their "core customers" by asking (1) Which customers are the most profitable and loyal, require less service, and seem to prefer stable, long-term relationships? (2) Which customers place the greatest value on what you offer? (3) Which customers are worth more to you than to your competitors?

Heskett, Sasser, and Schlesinger (1997) call this "potential-based marketing," combining measures of loyalty with data describing potential levels of usage. Companies then attempt to increase shares of purchases by customers who either value the services more than other customers or who show the greatest loyalty to a single provider. By lengthening relationships with the loyal customers, increasing sales with existing customers, and increasing the profitability on each sale opportunity, they thereby increase the potential of each customer. Few rigorous academic studies have yet been published documenting the moderating effect of tiers of customers on profits, although both Reichheld (1996a) and Blattberg and Deighton (1996) have offered arguments, heuristics, and methodologies for determining segment profitability. In one of the few academic studies demonstrating the importance of focusing on profitability with individual customers, Grant and Schlesinger (1995) estimated the full profit potential across tiers of customers. Using a Canadian grocery store context, they calculated the impact of expanding the customer base by 2% with primary shoppers: a profitability increase of more than 45%. Converting 200 secondary customers into primary customers would increase profits by 20%.

Overall, the evidence of the effects of service quality on profitability is emerging. As the variables involved have been delineated, and methodologies developed to study the associations among them, positive relationships have been found.

Electronic Service Quality

Jeff Bezos, founder and CEO of Amazon.com, a company that is arguably the pioneer in the field of e-commerce, had this to say about the role of service: "In the offline world . . . 30% of a company's resources are spent providing a good customer experience and 70% goes to marketing. But online . . . 70% should be devoted to creating a great customer experience and 30% should be spent on 'shouting' about it" (*Business Week*, March 22, 1999, p. EB 30). Unfortunately, considerable business evidence shows that few e-commerce sites have heeded Bezos' call. A study conducted by International Customer Service Association and e-Satisfy.com (2000) found that only 36% of customers are satisfied with their Internet purchasing experiences. Boston Consulting Group (2000) research shows that four out of five online purchasers have experienced one failed purchase (i.e., the system did not allow the purchase or the delivery was never fulfilled) and 28% of all online purchases fail. These failures disappoint consumers and have a detrimental impact on the future of electronic retailers: 28% of customers frustrated by their e-commerce experience report that they will not shop online again and 23% will not buy from the offending site again.

Traditional versus e-Service Quality

Are the findings about traditional service quality generalizable to electronic contexts (e-SQ)? Emerging research on the topics of technology and electronic service indicates that there are significant differences between the online and offline contexts. Insights from studies dealing with people-technology interactions imply that customer evaluation of new technologies is a unique process. For instance, findings from an extensive qualitative study of how customers interact with and evaluate technology-based products (Mick and Fournier 1995) suggest that (a) customer satisfaction with such products involves a highly complex, meaning-laden, long-term process, (b) the process might vary across different customer segments, and (c) satisfaction in such contexts is not always a function of pre-consumption comparison standards. Another major qualitative study by the same authors (Mick and Fournier 1998), focusing on peoples' reactions to technology, suggests that technology may trigger positive and negative feelings simultaneously. Moreover, other qualitative as well as empirical research demonstrates that customers' propensity to embrace new technologies (i.e., their *technology readiness*) depends on the relative dominance of positive and negative feelings in their overall technology beliefs (Parasuraman 2000).

A comparison of the way consumers evaluate SQ and e-SQ reveals differences in the role of expectations, number and nature of dimensions, and cognitive-emotional content. In addition, there seems to be a greater number of consumer tradeoffs and hence curvilinearity along e-SQ dimensions than in the case of SQ (Zeithaml, Parasuraman, and Malhotra 2000).

Expectations   There is evidence that expectations are not as well formed in e-SQ as they are in SQ. Focus group participants in a study of e-SQ (Zeithaml, Parasuraman, and Malhotra 2002) were unable to articulate their e-SQ expectations except when it came to issues of order fulfillment (e.g., having items in stock, delivering what is ordered, delivering when promised, and billing accuracy). Their difficulty expressing expectations about other dimensions is consistent with Mick and Fournier's (1995, 1998) conclusion, based on in-depth probing of consumer reactions to new technologies: "In buying and owning technological products, an individual's pre-consumption standards are often non-existent, weak, inaccurate, or subject to change as life circumstances shift" (1995, p. 1).

Personalization versus Personal Service (Empathy)   Personal service (the empathy dimension of SERVQUAL) is not critical in online service transactions. While customers seek understanding, reassurance, courtesy, and other aspects of personal attention in offline contexts, these service requirements seem to be key issues in perceived e-SQ only in service recovery or in highly complex decisions when customers sought special assistance (often on the telephone as follow-up). Many focus group participants were only interested in having efficient transactions.

Cognitive Evaluation   Compared to customers' assessment of SQ, e-SQ evaluation seems to be a more cognitive than emotional. Purchasing online appears to be a very goal-directed behavior: customers are interested in efficient transactions. While emotions such as anger and frustration were expressed when reporting on problems arising from online transactions, these appeared to be less intense than those associated with traditional service encounters (see Zeithaml, Parasuraman, and Malhotra 2002). Moreover, positive feelings of warmth or attachment that are engendered in SQ situations did not surface in the focus groups as characteristics of e-SQ experiences.

Measuring Electronic Service Quality

While commercial surveys of customer satisfaction with websites (e.g., BizRate.com surveys) have existed for several years, the published scholarly literature is limited. However, some academic researchers have developed scales to measure electronic service quality. Four scales in particular are worthy of mention.

Lociacono, Watson, and Goodhue (2000) created a WEBQUAL scale to help website designers create sites that positively affect the interaction perceptions of users. The WEBQUAL scale has 12 dimensions: informational fit to task, interaction, trust, response time, design, intuitiveness, visual appeal, innovativeness, flow-emotional appeal, integrated communication, business processes, and substitutability. Since the purpose of the scale was to influence interface design rather than measure service quality, some of the dimensions are irrelevant to perceived service quality (e.g., flow-emotional appeal, substitutability, and innovativeness), and several key dimensions related to service quality are omitted. An overall dimension called customer service was eliminated from the scale because it could not be measured. Finally, the scale was developed by having students visit websites to evaluate them rather than using actual purchasers and thus does not include fulfillment as a dimension.

Wolfinbarger and Gilly (2002) used online and offline focus groups, a sorting task, and an online survey of a customer panel to develop a scale called .comQ (later relabeled eTailQ [Wolfinbarger and Gilly 2003]). The scale contains four dimensions: *website design* (involving design attributes as well as an item dealing with personalization), *reliability/fulfillment* (involving accurate product representation, on-time delivery, and accurate orders), *privacy/security* (feeling safe and trusting of the site), and *customer service* (combining interest in solving problems, personnel's willingness to help, and prompt answers to inquiries). Drawing on both the service quality and retailing literatures, their scale contains 14 attributes in these four factors. Although Wolfinbarger and Gilly's goal is excellent and their three-study approach comprehensive, the resulting scale raises several questions. While two of their dimensions (privacy/security and reliability/fulfillment) show strong face validity and are highly descriptive of the items they represent, the other two dimensions (website design and customer service) appear less internally consistent and distinct. These dimensions, as well as other items that might be relevant to customer assessment of service quality on websites, need to be tested further.

Zeithaml, Parasuraman, and Malhotra's (2001) study dealt specifically with how customers assess e-SQ as well as with the antecedents and consequences of e-SQ. In that research, e-SQ is defined as the extent to which a website facilitates efficient and effective shopping, purchasing, and delivery. In exploratory research involving focus groups of experienced and inexperienced users, consumers reported that they used 11 dimensions to evaluate e-SQ: access, ease of navigation, efficiency, flexibility, reliability, personalization, security/privacy, responsiveness, assurance/trust, site aesthetics, and price knowledge.

The empirical phase of the research involved the development of a scale to measure e-SQ, administration of the scale, then scale-reduction/refinement analyses (Parasuraman, Zeithaml, and Malhotra 2004). The analysis resulted in a core e-service quality scale with 22 items on four dimensions:

Efficiency: the ease and speed of accessing and using the site
Fulfillment: the extent to which the site's promises about order delivery and item availability are fulfilled
Reliability: the degree to which the site's technical function performs correctly
Privacy: the degree to which the site is safe and protects customer information

The analysis also resulted in an e-recovery service quality scale consisting of 11 items on three dimensions.

Responsiveness: the degree to which problems and returns are successfully handled through the site

Compensation: the degree to which customers are compensated for problems

Contact: the degree to which help can be accessed by telephone or online representatives

Dimensions and Perceptual Attributes: SQ versus e-SQ

In comparing the dimensions of traditional SQ and e-SQ, it is clear that some are similar and some are different. Reliability and responsiveness are shared dimensions, but new Internet-specific dimensions appear to be critical in that context. Efficiency and fulfillment are core dimensions in e-SQ. Even though the attributes of fulfillment are similar to the attributes of reliability for the SERVQUAL scale, the way they group together when customers form judgments differs.

Second, as reported in Parasuraman, Zeithaml, and Malhotra (2004), customers cannot provide evaluations on the recovery dimensions unless they have experienced a problem or needed information beyond that presented on the site. The personal (i.e., friendly, empathetic, understanding) flavor of perceived SQ's empathy dimension is not required on the Internet except as it makes transactions more efficient or in non-routine situations.

Directions for Future Research

SERVQUAL Measurement Issues

The most recent refinements to SERVQUAL, and the empirical results from analyses conducted to reassess them, raise a number of issues for further investigation. First, although the three-column questionnaire format is superior to the two-column format (see appendices 3 and 4), especially in terms of diagnostic value, administering it in its entirety may pose practical difficulties, particularly in telephone surveys or when the list of generic items is supplemented with more context-specific items as suggested by PBZ (1991b). Therefore, it would be useful to explore the soundness of administering logical subsections of the questionnaire (e.g., sections pertaining to the five dimensions) to comparable sub-samples of customers so as to still achieve its full diagnostic value.

Second, research is needed to explore why the actual results from this study as well as earlier studies (cf. Brown, Churchill, and Peter 1993; PBZ 1993) apparently do not fully support the alleged psychometric deficiencies of difference-score measures of service quality. Such research might provide a more enlightened understanding of the pros and cons of using difference scores in service-quality measurement.

Third, based on the findings reported in this monograph and consistent with calls issued by PZB (1994b) and Perreault (1992), there is a need to explicitly incorporate practical criteria such as diagnostic value into the traditional scale-assessment paradigm that is dominated by psychometric criteria.

Fourth, as suggested by results from the study discussed in Appendix 3, direct measures of service quality may tend to produce upwardly biased ratings. This possibility warrants further exploration. Insights from research aimed at understanding the causes of this tendency and estimating the extent of upward bias it produces would be helpful in reducing the bias, or at least correcting for it in interpreting direct-measure ratings.

Fifth, additional research on the dimensionality of the SERVQUAL items is warranted. Although there is support for SERVQUAL's five-dimensional configuration, considerable interdimensional overlap has been found, especially among responsiveness, assurance, and empathy. PBZ (1991b) have speculated about possible reasons for this overlap and have proffered directions for future research on this issue. Research is also needed to uncover the underlying causes and managerial implications of the empirical correlations among the dimensions.

Finally, further empirical work is needed to evaluate and revise as necessary the preliminary scales developed thus far to measure customers' assessments of the core and recovery service quality of websites.

Consequences of Service Quality

Although the link between service quality and purchase intentions has been confirmed, the more compelling relationship between purchase intentions and *actual* purchase behavior has not. It is well known that customers are not particularly good predictors of their own behavior and tend to over-report their intentions to buy products and services. Further, the relationship between customer purchase intentions and *initial* purchase behavior will be one of the most difficult to document because it requires matching data from customers before purchase (usually obtained anonymously) with post-purchase data.

Post-purchase data can be collected through warranty cards or other means; however, to connect these data to pre-purchase intentions requires both customer identification and a mechanism to relate the two forms of data. One context where this connection might be observed is when electronic services surveys are disseminated before purchases are made. Using e-mail or other electronic coding, a company could query survey participants about the desirability of a given service, then follow up to see if they purchase the service.

Other issues pertaining to the impact of service quality and worthy of further research include:

How Does Service Compare in Effectiveness to Other Retention Strategies Such as Price?   Statistical analysis is needed to allow researchers to examine the relative contribution of different marketing variables to retention. To date no studies have incorporated all or most potential explanatory variables to examine their relative importance in keeping customers. A number of methodologies could be appropriate for studying this question, including consumer questionnaires that examine the explained variance of customers' remaining with companies as a function of their assessments of companies' marketing mix. Many companies actually have survey data containing these variables but have either not analyzed the data for this purpose or have not reported their findings.

What Aspects of Service Are Most Important for Customer Retention?   The only studies that have examined specific aspects of service and their impact on customer retention have been early studies looking at customer complaint management (Fornell and Wernerfelt 1987, 1988). A decade ago this was appropriate, as service was often equated with customer service, the after-sale function that dealt with dissatisfied customers. However, service is multi-faceted, consisting of a wide variety of customer-perceived dimensions including reliability, responsiveness, and empathy and resulting from innumerable company strategies such as technology and process improvement.

In research exploring the relative importance of service dimensions on overall service quality or customer satisfaction, the bulk of the findings confirms that reliability is most critical (PZB 1988; Boulding, Kalra, Staelin, and Zeithaml 1993, ZBP 1996), although others have demonstrated the importance of customization (Fornell, Johnson, Anderson, Cha, and Bryant 1996) and other factors. Because the dimensions and attributes are delivered in many cases with totally different internal strategies, resources must be allocated where they are most needed, and studies on this topic could provide direction.

What Are the Relative Impacts of Traditional and Electronic Service Quality on Customers Touched by Both?   While research to date suggests similarities between traditional and electronic service quality, it also suggests some important differences. As such, a fruitful area for further research is to understand the process through which customers assess the overall service image of companies that interact with customers through both conventional and electronic channels.

A key managerial research need is a measurement scale that can be used to capture service quality both in online and offline channels for the same company. Given the differences between SQ and e-SQ, this may be difficult, yet it would be valuable for managers to be able to compare their online and offline service quality.

Electronic Service Quality

Further empirical testing of e-SQ scales is needed. All scales currently under development—including WebQual, .comQ/eTailQ, and e-SERVQUAL—should be examined for their psychometric properties and diagnostic value and improved where needed.

When concepts and measures of e-SQ have been developed, it will be possible to investigate questions about the importance of different dimensions and perceptual attributes to overall electronic service quality and its consequences. We know from nearly 20 years of research that reliability is the most important dimension of traditional service quality, and we need to understand what dimensions are most responsible for driving electronic service quality. Because the limited conceptual development of e-SQ suggests that reliability consists of attributes that are different from those for SQ, the importance of reliability relative to other dimensions needs to be reassessed in this context. Other tradeoffs are important to investigate, such as the tradeoff between e-SQ and price in contributing to perceptions of overall value, intentions to purchase, and actual purchase.

Building on the foundation of the needed research discussed above, additional research is needed to empirically address the question of where to invest in electronic service quality improvement. Should it be core or recovery service? What actions on a website most affect the identified key drivers of revisits or repurchase? A framework such as return on service quality (Rust, Zahorik, and Keiningham 1994) would be useful in determining where to invest.

A topic in great need of research is personalization/customization of websites. When is personalization viewed as being efficient and when is it viewed as being intrusive? What types of personalization and customization (such as receiving e-mails from the company) are seen as time consuming and what types (such as not needing to input information) are viewed as time saving? How do consumers respond to the different approaches to personalization and customization? Can customers distinguish among types of personalization that are based on remembering individual customer data and those that are driven by techniques to identify similarities across customers? Are these approaches drivers of e-SQ or not?

We know almost nothing about the demographic, behavioral, and experience correlates of e-SQ. Does age, gender, or income of customers affect their perceptions of service quality delivery through websites? How is experience with websites related? Are there other behavioral correlates that influence perceptions? All of these questions remain to be investigated.

One area of research that has potential for surfacing rich insights is the examination of the inter-relationships among technology readiness, e-SQ, and e-shopping behavior. Zeithaml, Parasuraman, and Malhotra (2002) provide a model and propositions and call for testing of these relationships.

Appendix 1. SERVQUAL Development and Refinement

Construction of SERVQUAL

Drawing upon insights and examples from extensive focus group interviews, PZB (1988) developed a set of 97 statements representing various specific facets of the 10 service quality dimensions. These statements formed the basis for a two-part instrument consisting of 97 expectations statements and 97 corresponding perceptions statements. In accordance with recommended procedures for scale development (Churchill 1979), roughly half of the expectations statements and the corresponding perceptions statements were worded negatively.

To purify the initial instrument, PZB administered it to a sample of 200 customers representing five service categories—appliance repair and maintenance, retail banking, long-distance telephone, securities brokerage, and credit cards. Analyses of the perception-minus-expectation gap scores on the 97 items resulted in a more parsimonious 34-item instrument with statements grouped into seven dimensions. (The analyses included item-to-total correlation analysis, factor analysis, and assessment of internal consistency of items in each dimension.)

To further assess the reliability, validity, and dimensionality of the 34-item instrument, PZB used it to collect data pertaining to the service quality of four nationally known, U.S.-based companies (a bank, a company offering appliance repair and maintenance services, a credit card company, and a long-distance telephone company). Four independent samples, consisting of 200 customers from each the four companies, participated in this research phase. Results of analyses (similar to those mentioned above) of the perception-expectation gap scores were consistent across the four samples. These findings resulted in: (1) further elimination of items to create a 22-item instrument and (2) grouping of the 22 items into five general dimensions. Strong evidence supporting the reliability, validity, and dimensionality of this condensed instrument—labeled SERVQUAL—is documented in PZB (1988). A complete listing of the 22-item statements in the two parts of SERVQUAL, as well as instructions for the two parts, is also provided in PZB (1988) and in Appendix 2.

Refinement of SERVQUAL

In a multi-sector study discussed in PBZ (1991b), SERVQUAL was further refined by measuring customer assessments of service quality for telephone repair, retail banking, and insurance services. Five nationally known companies—one telephone company, two insurance companies, and two banks—participated. The refinements to SERVQUAL were initially suggested by results from a pretest of the original (1988) version in a mail survey of 300 customers of the participating telephone company. The refined SERVQUAL was then tested through mail surveys of independent samples of customers of each of the five companies. The refinements and brief rationales for them are outlined below (a more detailed discussion is available in PBZ 1991b).

The distribution of expectations ratings obtained in the pretest was highly skewed toward the upper end of the 7-point scale (mean expectation score was 6.22). Suspecting that the "should" terminology in the expectations statements might be responsible for the high ratings, the statements were revised to capture what customers *will* expect from companies delivering *excellent* service. For example, the original expectations statement, "Banks *should* give customers individual attention," was revised to read, "*Excellent* banks *will* give customers individual attention." The instructions for the expectations section were also appropriately altered.

The negatively worded statements in the original SERVQUAL instrument were problematic for several reasons: (1) they were awkward, (2) they confused respondents (the pre-test data showed substantially higher standard deviations for the negatively worded statements than for those worded positively), and (3) they seemed to lower the reliabilities (coefficient alpha values) for the dimensions containing them. Therefore, all negatively worded statements were changed to a positive format.

Finally, two original items—one each under tangibles and assurance—were replaced with two new items to reduce redundancy and to more fully capture the dimensions. These changes also reflected suggestions from company managers who reviewed the pre-test questionnaire.

The psychometric properties of the refined SERVQUAL instrument were reassessed with data from the five companies. The results indicated strong reliability for the five multiple-item components of the instrument:

across the five companies, the coefficient alpha values ranged from .80 to .86 for tangibles, .88 to .92 for reliability, .88 to .93 for responsiveness, .87 to .91 for assurance, and .85 to .89 for empathy. The five components also possessed high predictive and convergent validity, as indicated by their ability to explain the variance in customers' perceptions of the companies' overall service quality. Regression analyses in which overall service quality (measured on a 10-point scale) was the dependent variable and the mean perception-expectation gap scores on the five SERVQUAL dimensions were the independent variables yielded adjusted R-squared values ranging from .57 to .71 across the five companies.

The evidence of reliability and validity reported above was stronger than the corresponding results obtained for the original SERVQUAL instrument (PZB 1988), indicating improved cohesiveness of the items under each dimension and demonstrating the ability of gap scores on the dimensions to predict overall service quality. However, results of factor analyses of the gap scores obtained from the refined instrument revealed somewhat greater overlap among the five dimensions—especially responsiveness and assurance—than in the case of the original SERVQUAL. Thus, the discriminant validity or uniqueness of the five components of the refined SERVQUAL instrument is in question.

Appendix 2. SERVQUAL Instrument

Note: In what follows, telephone repair services are used as an illustrative context.

Expectations Section

Directions: Based on your experiences as a customer of telephone repair services, please think about the kind of telephone company that would deliver excellent quality of repair service. Think about the kind of telephone company with which you would be pleased to do business. Please show the extent to which you think such a telephone company would possess the feature described by each statement. If you feel a feature is *not at all essential* for excellent telephone companies such as the one you have in mind, circle the number "1." If you feel a feature is *absolutely essential* for excellent telephone companies, circle "7." If your feelings are less strong, circle one of the numbers in the middle. There are no right or wrong answers—all we are interested in is a number that truly reflects your feelings regarding telephone companies that would deliver excellent quality of service.

Note: Each of the statements was accompanied by a 7-point scale anchored at the ends by the labels "strongly disagree" (= 1) and "strongly agree" (= 7). Intermediate scale points were not labeled. Also, the headings (tangibles, reliability, etc.), shown here to indicate which statements fall under each dimension, were not included in the actual questionnaire.

Tangibles

1. Excellent telephone companies will have modern-looking equipment.
2. The physical facilities at excellent telephone companies will be visually appealing.
3. Employees of excellent telephone companies will be neat-appearing.
4. Materials associated with the service (such as pamphlets or statements) will be visually appealing in excellent telephone companies.

Reliability

5. When excellent telephone companies promise to do something by a certain time, they will do so.

6. When customers have a problem, excellent telephone companies will show a sincere interest in solving it.

7. Excellent telephone companies will perform the service right the first time.

8. Excellent telephone companies will provide their services at the time they promise to do so.

9. Excellent telephone companies will insist on error-free records.

Responsiveness

10. Employees of excellent telephone companies will tell customers exactly when services will be performed.

11. Employees of excellent telephone companies will give prompt service to customers.

12. Employees of excellent telephone companies will always be willing to help customers.

13. Employees of excellent telephone companies will never be too busy to respond to customer requests.

Assurance

14. The behavior of employees of excellent telephone companies will instill confidence in customers.

15. Customers of excellent telephone companies will feel safe in their transactions.

16. Employees of excellent telephone companies will be consistently courteous with customers.

17. Employees of excellent telephone companies will have the knowledge to answer customer questions.

Empathy

18. Excellent telephone companies will give customers individual attention.

19. Excellent telephone companies will have operating hours convenient to all their customers.

20. Excellent telephone companies will have employees who give customers personal attention.

21. Excellent telephone companies will have the customers' best interests at heart.

22. The employees of excellent telephone companies will understand the specific needs of their customers.

Perceptions Section

Directions: The following set of statements relates to your feelings about XYZ Telephone Company's repair service. For each statement, please show the extent to which you believe XYZ has the feature described by the statement. Once again, circling a "1" means that you strongly disagree that XYZ has that feature, and circling a "7" means that you strongly agree. You may circle any of the numbers in the middle that show how strong your feelings are. There are no right or wrong answers—all that we are interested in is a number that best shows your perceptions about XYZ's repair service.

Note: Each of the statements was accompanied by a 7-point scale anchored at the ends by the labels "strongly disagree" (= 1) and "strongly agree" (= 7). Intermediate scale points were not labeled. Also, the headings (tangibles, reliability, etc.), shown here to indicate which statements fall under each dimension, were not included in the actual questionnaire.

Tangibles

1. XYZ has modern-looking equipment.

2. XYZ's physical facilities are visually appealing.

3. XYZ's employees are neat-appearing.

4. Materials associated with the service (such as pamphlets or statements) are visually appealing at XYZ.

Reliability

5. When XYZ promises to do something by a certain time, it does so.

6. When you have a problem, XYZ shows a sincere interest in solving it.

7. XYZ performs the service right the first time.

8. XYZ provides its services at the time it promises to do so.

9. XYZ insists on error-free records.

Responsiveness

10. Employees of XYZ tell you exactly when services will be performed.

11. Employees of XYZ give you prompt service.

12. Employees of XYZ are always willing to help you.

13. Employees of XYZ are never too busy to respond to your requests.

Assurance

14. The behavior of employees of XYZ instills confidence in customers.

15. You feel safe in your transactions with XYZ.

16. Employees of XYZ are consistently courteous with you.

17. Employees of XYZ have the knowledge to answer your questions.

Empathy

18. XYZ gives you individual attention.

19. XYZ has operating hours convenient to all its customers.

20. XYZ has employees who give you personal attention.

21. XYZ has your best interests at heart.

22. Employees of XYZ understand your specific needs.

Point-Allocation Question

Directions: Listed below are five features pertaining to telephone companies and the repair services they offer. We would like to know how important each of these features is to *you* when you evaluate a telephone company's quality of repair service. Please allocate a total of 100 points among the five features *according to how important each feature is to you*—the more important a feature is to you, the more points you should allocate to it. Please ensure that the points you allocate to the five features add up to 100.

The appearance of the telephone company's physical facilities, equipment, personnel, and communications materials. _____ points

The ability of the telephone company to perform the promised service dependably and accurately. _____ points

The willingness of the telephone company to help customers and provide prompt service. _____ points

The knowledge and courtesy of the telephone company's employees and their ability to convey trust and confidence._____ points

The caring, individualized attention the telephone company provides its customers_____ points

Total Points Allocated: 100 points

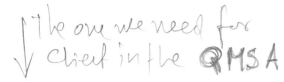
The one we need for Client in the QMSA

Appendix 3. A Multi-Sector Study to Expand and Further Test SERVQUAL

PZB (1994b) conducted a multi-sector study to (1) augment SERVQUAL to incorporate the measure of service superiority (MSS) and the measure of service adequacy (MSA) corresponding to the desired and adequate expectation levels in an expanded conceptual model of service expectations (ZBP 1993) and (2) assess the relative merits and demerits of the difference-score and direct operationalizations of the service quality gap measures (i.e., MSS and MSA). This study tested two measurement formats (both formats can be found in Appendix 4):

Three-Column Format

This format involves obtaining separate ratings of desired, adequate, and perceived service with three identical, side-by-side scales, requiring the computation of differences between ratings to quantify MSS and MSA. Its operationalization of service quality is similar to that of SERVQUAL except that the scales appear side by side, eliminating the need to repeat the battery of items.

22 items only

Two-Column Format

Unlike SERVQUAL which used difference scores, this format obtained *direct* ratings of MSS and MSA with two identical, side-by-side scales. The questionnaires used in the study contained the full battery of items in Appendix 2. In addition, the term *minimum service* rather than *adequate service* was used in the questionnaires based on the recommendation of customers in focus groups that pre-tested earlier questionnaire drafts.

The two questionnaire formats were used in mail surveys of independent samples of customers from four large companies in the United States—a computer manufacturer, a retail chain, an auto insurance company, and a life insurance company.

Results

Consistent with findings from earlier studies, the perceptions-only ratings (obtained from the third column of the three-column format) had

53

the most predictive power. Specifically, regressing customer ratings on a 9-point, overall service quality scale on the perceptions scores on the five SERVQUAL dimensions yielded R-squared values ranging from .72 to .86 across the four companies. In contrast, when difference-score ratings of MSS (i.e., perception-minus-desired service ratings) on the five dimensions were used as independent variables in the regression analyses, the R-squared values ranged from .51 to .60 across companies. When direct ratings of MSS (from the two-column format questionnaire) were used as independent variables the R-squared values ranged from .45 to .74 across companies. Thus, measuring perceptions alone should suffice if the sole purpose of service quality measurement on individual attributes is to try to maximize the explained variance in overall service ratings.

However, from a practitioner's standpoint, an equally important purpose is to pinpoint service quality shortfalls and take appropriate corrective action. From this *diagnostic-value* perspective, it is prudent to measure perceptions against expectations. This was evident from several patterns of results for the four companies. For instance, consider the following mean ratings (on a 9-point scale) obtained for the computer company on the reliability and tangibles dimensions:

	Desired Service	Adequate Service	Perceptions
Reliability	8.5	7.2	7.5
Tangibles	7.5	6.0	7.5

On the basis of perceptions ratings alone, the company's performance is identical on both dimensions and, as such, the company may place the same level of service-improvement emphasis on each. That such a strategy will be suboptimal becomes evident when the perceptions ratings are interpreted in conjunction with the desired- and adequate-service expectations. Performance on tangibles far exceeds the adequate service level [the MSA rating is 1.5] and actually meets the desired service level [the MSS rating is 0]. In contrast, performance on reliability barely exceeds the adequate service level [the MSA rating is .3] and is substantially short of the desired service level [the MSS rating is –1]. Clearly, devoting equal attention to both dimensions would be wasteful; instead, the company should give far higher priority to improving performance on reliability.

Thus, measuring expectations is warranted from the standpoint of being able to pinpoint the most serious service shortfalls and make wise resource-allocation decisions. Before expending effort to make improvements on any service attribute, a company should ascertain, at a minimum, whether perceived performance on the attribute falls below, within, or above the customers' zone of tolerance. Such a comparative assessment is not possible if perceptions alone are measured.

In another example in PZB's (1994b) multi-sector study, the retail-chain customers' mean perceptions ratings on the 9-point scale for reliability, responsiveness, assurance, empathy, and tangibles were 6.6, 6.2, 6.7, 6.2, and 7.2, respectively.

	Desired Service	Adequate Service	Perceptions
Reliability		7.1	6.6
Responsiveness		6.6	6.2
Assurance		6.9	6.7
Empathy		6.6	6.2
Tangibles		6.6	7.2

Although these ratings suggest room for improvement, the chain might still consider them to be "decent" ratings, especially since even the lowest rating of 6.2 is more than a full point above the scale's midpoint of 5. However, the adequate service ratings for reliability, responsiveness, assurance, empathy, and tangibles were 7.1, 6.6, 6.9, 6.6, and 6.6, respectively. Thus, except on the dimension of tangibles, the retail chain's perceived performance does not even meet customers' minimum expectations. The retail chain's service quality is much worse than what one might infer from the perceptions ratings alone.

The results from the study also shed light on whether increased questionnaire length due to measuring expectations adversely affects response rate. Both the two-column and three-column format questionnaires (shown in Appendix 4) are physically shorter than the two-part SERVQUAL (shown in Appendix 2) because they do not repeat the battery of items. However, the two-column format is "shorter" than the three-column format in that the former requires one less set of ratings.

Thus, if questionnaire length (reflected by the number of sets of ratings respondents are requested to provide) has a detrimental effect on response rate, one would predict a higher response rate for the two-column format than for the three-column format. The actual response rates obtained run counter to this prediction—in all four companies the response rate for the three-column format was equal to or higher than the response rate for the two-column format (the mean response rates across companies for the two-column and three-column formats were 22% and 24%, respectively). These results suggest that measuring expectations separately is not likely to lower response rates.

New Evidence: How Should the Expectations Construct Be Operationalized?

Although the results of the study do not directly address this issue, they provide support for the meaningfulness of using the zone of tolerance (bounded by the desired and adequate service expectations) as a yardstick against which to compare perceived service performance. As implied by the illustrative findings discussed above, operationalizing customer expectations as a zone or range of service levels is not only feasible empirically but also valuable from a diagnostic standpoint. Using the zone of tolerance as a comparison standard in evaluating service performance can help companies in understanding how well they are meeting at least customers' minimum requirements, and how much improvement is needed before they achieve the status of service superiority.

New Evidence: Is It Appropriate to Operationalize Service Quality as a Difference Score?

As already discussed, while the two-column format measures the gap between perceptions and expectations *directly*, the three-column format involves operationalizing the gap as a difference score. Therefore, relevant results from the comparative study can be used to assess the reliability, validity, and diagnostic value of the direct and difference-score measures.

Based on values of coefficient alpha—the conventional criterion for assessing the reliability (or internal consistency) of items making up a scale—both the direct and difference-score measures of service quality fared well. For instance, the range of coefficient alpha values across companies for the five SERVQUAL dimensions (based on the MSS scores representing the measure of service superiority or the gap between perceptions and desired-service expectations) were as follows:

	Direct Measure	Difference-Score Measure
Reliability	.90 to .96	.87 to .95
Responsiveness	.83 to .95	.84 to .91
Assurance	.88 to .94	.81 to .90
Empathy	.91 to .97	.85 to .93
Tangibles	.88 to .97	.75 to .88

As the above results indicate, although the reliability coefficients are somewhat higher for the direct measure, all the values for the difference-score measure exceed the lower threshold value of .7 suggested by Nunnally (1978). However, some concern has been raised in the psychometric literature about the appropriateness of computing coefficient alphas for difference scores, and an alternative formula has been recommended specifically for assessing the reliability of a difference-score measure (Peter, Churchill, and Brown 1993). The reliability coefficients obtained through this formula for the difference-score operationalization of MSS were somewhat lower than the coefficient alpha values reported above, but were still quite high. In fact, the coefficient values for the SERVQUAL dimensions across all companies exceeded .8 with just two exceptions in one company (the coefficients for assurance and tangibles in the computer company were .71 and .65, respectively). Thus, the reliability of the difference-score operationalization of service quality, although lower than that of the direct measure, seems acceptable.

Both the direct and the difference-score measures of service quality have *face validity* in that both are consistent with the conceptual definition of service quality as the discrepancy between perceptions and expectations. And, as implied by the regression results reported earlier, both measures have good *predictive validity*—the R-squared values for the regressions with overall quality as the dependent variable range from .45 to .74 for the direct measure and .51 to .60 for the difference-score measure.

service quality is proposed in the literature to be an
t of _perceived value_ (e.g., Zeithaml 1988), one can assess the
nomological validity of the service quality measures by the degree to
which they are related to perceived value. In the present study, customers
rated the "overall value for the money" offered by their respective companies on a 9-point scale. As in the case of the overall quality ratings, the
overall value ratings for each company were regressed on the MSS scores
for the five SERVQUAL dimensions. The range of R-squared values from
these regression analyses was .34 to .57 for the direct measure and .31 to
.58 for the difference-score measure. These results support the nomolog-
ical validity of both measures. Moreover, comparing these ranges of R-
squared values for the value regressions with the corresponding ranges
reported above for the quality regressions reveals that the variance
explained is higher for quality, the construct the direct and difference-
score formats purport to measure, than for value, a different construct.
This pattern of results offers some support for the _discriminant validity_
of both measures as well.

The two measures did differ in terms of possible _response error_, a
potential threat to their validity. Response error was assessed by examining the logical consistency of the MSA and MSS ratings from the two-
column format and of the adequate-service and desired-service ratings
from the three-column format. An instance of response error occurs
when the MSA rating on an item exceeds the MSS rating, or when the
adequate-service rating exceeds the desired-service rating. The percentages of respondents who committed one or more such errors ranged
from 8.6% to 18.2% for the two-column format, and from .6% to 2.7%
for the three-column format. Thus, the validity threat due to possible
response error is far greater for the direct measure than for the difference-score measure.

The study's results also suggested a need for caution in interpreting the
direct-measure ratings because of possible upward bias in them. To illus-
trate, with just two exceptions, the mean values for the direct measures of
service superiority (i.e., MSS) along the five SERVQUAL dimensions were
greater than 5, the scale point at which the desired and perceived service
levels are equal (the exceptions were mean ratings of 4.9 and 5.0 for the
retail chain's responsiveness and empathy, respectively). This consistent

pattern implied that perceived service performance was *above* the desired service level for virtually all dimensions in each company. In contrast, except for tangibles in the computer company, the difference-score values of MSS were negative, implying that perceived service performance was *below* the desired service level. Given that the desired service level represents a form of *ideal* standard, perceived performance falling below that level (on at least several dimensions) seems a more plausible and face-valid finding than a consistent pattern of perceptions exceeding the desired service level. As such, the direct measures may be producing upwardly biased ratings that can mislead executives into believing that their companies' service performance is better than it actually is.

From a practical or diagnostic-value standpoint, the three-column format questionnaire (from which the difference-score measures are derived) has yet another advantage—by virtue of its generating separate ratings of the adequate-service, desired-service, and perception levels, this format is capable of *pinpointing* the position of the zone of tolerance and the perceived service level relative to the zone. The direct measures obtained from the two-column format questionnaire can indicate whether the perceived service level is above the tolerance zone (MSS score greater than 5), below the tolerance zone (MSA score less than 5), or within the tolerance zone (MSS score less than or equal to 5 and MSA score greater than or equal to 5). However, ratings from the two-column format cannot identify the tolerance zone's position on a continuum of expectation levels; nor can they pinpoint the perceived service level relative to the zone.

In summary, the difference-score operationalization of service quality appears to have psychometric properties that are as sound as those of the direct-measure operationalization. Moreover, the three-column format questionnaire yields richer diagnostics than the two-column format questionnaire. Thus, operationalizing service quality as difference scores seems appropriate.

New Evidence: Does SERVQUAL Have Five Distinct Dimensions That Transcend Different Contexts?

To verify the dimensionality of the direct-measure and difference-score versions of SERVQUAL, the MSA and MSS scores on the individual items were factor-analyzed to extract five factors. The results showed that for both questionnaire versions the reliability items formed a distinct factor. The responsiveness, assurance, and empathy items primarily loaded on the same factor. The tangibles items, though distinct from the other dimensions, were split among the three remaining factors. The splitting of tangibles into several factors has occurred in past studies as well (PBZ 1991b) and might be an artifact of extracting five factors (i.e., because the items for the other four dimensions were captured by just two factors, the tangibles items may have split up to represent the remaining factors).

To further evaluate the distinctiveness of the SERVQUAL dimensions, confirmatory factor analyses were conducted using LISREL to assess the tenability of two alternative measurement models. One was a five-construct model in which the items loaded on the five SERVQUAL dimensions according to the a priori groupings of the items. The second model was a three-construct model in which the reliability and tangibles items loaded on two distinct constructs, while the remaining items loaded on the third construct (acknowledging the possible unidimensionality of responsiveness, assurance, and empathy). The analyses showed both models to be defensible on the basis of the traditional criteria of GFI (goodness-of-fit index), AGFI (adjusted GFI), and RMSR (root-mean-squared residual). Additional analyses conducted to assess the *relative* fit of the two models and to explore further the distinctiveness of the five dimensions provided stronger support for the five-dimensional structure than for the three-dimensional structure (details of these analyses are available in PZB 1994b). In summary, although the results showed evidence of discriminant validity among SERVQUAL's five dimensions, they also support the possibility of a three-dimensional structure where responsiveness, assurance, and empathy meld into a single factor.

Appendix 4. SERVQUAL: Two Formats

Note: Both formats are for the auto insurer (one of four companies that participated in the study) and only one illustrative item is shown in each.

Two-Column Format

Please think about the quality of service _____ offers compared to the two different levels of service defined below:

Minimum service level—the minimum level of service performance you consider adequate
Desired service level—the level of service performance you desire

For each of the following statements, please indicate: (a) how _____'s performance compares with your minimum service level by circling one of the numbers in the first column; and (b) how _____'s performance compares with your desired service level by circling one of the numbers in the second column.

When it comes to prompt service to policyholders

Compared to my minimum service level, ____'s service performance is:								Compared to my desired service level, ____'s service performance is:							
Low					High		No opinion	Low					High		No opinion
1	2	3	4	5	6	7	N	1	2	3	4	5	6	7	N

Three-Column Format

We would like your impressions about _____'s service performance relative to your expectations. Please think about the two different levels of expectations defined below:

Minimum service level—the minimum level of service performance you consider adequate
Desired service level—the level of service performance you desire

For each of the following statements, please indicate: (a) your minimum service level by circling one of the numbers in the first column; and (b) your desired service level by circling one of the numbers in the second column; and (c) your perception of _____'s service by circling one of the numbers in the third column.

When it comes to prompt service to policyholders

My minimum service level is:	My desired service level is:	My perception of _____'s service performance is:
Low High	Low High	Low High
1 2 3 4 5 6 7 8 9	1 2 3 4 5 6 7 8 9	1 2 3 4 5 6 7 8 9

Notes

1. Analytical and other details concerning these potential applications are available in ZPB (1990, pp. 175–80).
2. These questions relate to the need for SERVQUAL's expectations component (e.g., Babakus and Mangold 1992; Cronin and Taylor 1992), the interpretation and operationalization of expectations (Teas 1993), the reliability and validity of SERVQUAL's *difference-score* formulation (e.g., Babakus and Boller 1992; Brown, Churchill, and Peter 1993), and SERVQUAL's dimensionality (e.g., Carman 1990; Finn and Lamb 1991). In response to these questions, PZB have presented counterarguments, clarifications, and additional evidence to reaffirm the instrument's psychometric soundness and practical value (PBZ 1991b, 1993; PZB 1994a).

References

Aaker, David A., and Robert Jacobson (1994), "The Financial Information Content of Perceived Quality." *Journal of Marketing Research* 31 (May), 191–201.

Andaleeb, Syed Saad, and A. K. Basu (1998), "Do Warranties Influence Perceptions of Service Quality? A Study of the Automobile Repair and Service Industry." *Journal of Retailing and Consumer Services* 5 (2), 87–92.

Babakus, Emin, and Gregory W. Boller (1992), "An Empirical Assessment of the SERVQUAL Scale." *Journal of Business Research* 24 (3), 253–68.

Babakus, Emin, and W. Glynn Mangold (1992), "Adapting the SERVQUAL Scale to Hospital Services: An Empirical Investigation." *Health Services Research* 26 (6), 767–86.

Bell, David E., and Donald M. Leavitt (1998), "Bronner Slosberg Humphrey." Harvard Business School Case No. 9-598-136.

Berry, Leonard L. (1983), "Relationship Marketing." In *Emerging Perspectives on Services Marketing*, eds. Leonard L. Berry, G. Lynn Shostack, and Gregory D. Upah, 25–8. Chicago, Ill.: American Marketing Association.

Berry, Leonard L., and A. Parasuraman (1991), "Marketing to Employees." In *Marketing Services: Competing Through Quality*, chap. 9. New York, N.Y.: The Free Press.

Berry, Leonard L., and A. Parasuraman (1997), "Listening to the Customer: The Concept of a Service-Quality Information System." *Sloan Management Review* 38 (3) (Spring), 65–76.

Bettencourt, Lance A., and Kevin Gwinner (1996), "Customization of the Service Experience: The Role of the Frontline Employee." *International Journal of Service Industry Management* 7 (2), 3–20.

Bitner, Mary Jo (1993), "Managing the Evidence of Service." In *The Service Quality Handbook*, eds. Eberhard E. Scheuing and William F. Christopher, 358–70. New York, N.Y.: American Management Association.

Bitner, Mary Jo, Bernard H. Booms, and Mary Stanfield Tetreault (1990), "The Service Encounter: Diagnosing Favorable and Unfavorable Incidents." *Journal of Marketing* 54 (1) (January), 71–84.

Blattberg, Robert C., and John Deighton (1996), "Manage Marketing by the Customer Equity Test." *Harvard Business Review* 74 (July-August), 136–44.

Bojanic, David C. (1991), "Quality Measurement in Professional Services Firms." *Journal of Professional Services Marketing* 7 (2), 27–36.

Bolton, Ruth N., and James H. Drew (1991a), "A Longitudinal Analysis of the Impact of Service Changes on Customer Attitudes." *Journal of Marketing* 55 (1) (January), 1–9.

Bolton, Ruth N., and James H. Drew (1991b), "A Multistage Model of Customers' Assessments of Service Quality and Value." *Journal of Consumer Research* 17 (4) (March), 375–84.

Bongiorno, Lori (1993), "Franchise Fracas." *Business Week* (March 22), 68.

Bonner, P. Greg, and Richard Nelson (1985), "Product Attributes and Perceived Quality: Foods." In *Perceived Quality: How Consumers View Stores and Merchandise*, eds. J. Jacoby and J. Olson, 64–79. Lexington, Mass.: Lexington Books.

Boston Consulting Group (2000), http://www.nua.ie/surveys/index.cgi?f =VS&art_id=905355643&rel=true (retrieved February 17, 2004).

Boulding, William, Ajay Kalra, Richard Staelin, and Valarie Zeithaml (1993), "A Dynamic Process Model of Service Quality: From Expectations to Behavioral Intentions." *Journal of Marketing Research* 30 (February), 7–27.

Boulding, William, Richard Staelin, Ajay Kalra, and Valarie A. Zeithaml (1992), "Conceptualizing and Testing a Dynamic Process Model of Service Quality." Cambridge, Mass.: Marketing Science Institute, Report No. 92–121.

Bounds, Greg, Lyle Yorks, Mel Adams, and Gipsie Ranney (1994), *Beyond Total Quality Management toward the Emerging Paradigm*. New York, N.Y.: McGraw-Hill.

Bowen, David E. (1986), "Managing Customers as Human Resources." *Human Resource Management* 25 (3), 371–83.

Bowen, David E., and Edward E. Lawler III (1992), "The Empowerment of Service Workers: What, Why, How, and When." *Sloan Management Review* 33 (3) (Spring), 31–9.

Brensinger, Ronald P., and Douglas M. Lambert (1990), "Can the SERVQUAL Scale Be Generalized to Business-to-Business Services?" In *Knowledge Development in Marketing, 1990 AMA's Summer Educators' Conference Proceedings*, 289. Chicago, Ill.: American Marketing Association.

Brown, Stephen W., and Teresa A. Swartz (1989), "A Gap Analysis of Professional Service Quality." *Journal of Marketing* 53 (2) (April), 92–8.

Brown, Tom J., Gilbert A. Churchill, Jr., and J. Paul Peter (1993), "Improving the Measurement of Service Quality." *Journal of Retailing* 69 (Spring), 127–39.

Brucks, Merrie, Valarie A. Zeithaml, and Gillian Naylor (2000), "Price and Brand Name as Indicators of Quality Dimensions for Consumer Durables." *Journal of the Academy of Marketing Science* 28 (Summer), 359–74.

Buzzell, Richard D., and Bradley T. Gale (1987), *The PIMS Principles: Linking Strategy to Performance*. New York, N.Y.: The Free Press.

Camp, Robert (1989), *Benchmarking: The Search for Industry Best Practices That Lead to Superior Performance*. Milwaukee, Wisc.: American Society for Quality Control.

Carman, James M. (1990), "Consumer Perceptions of Service Quality: An Assessment of the SERVQUAL Dimensions." *Journal of Retailing* 66 (Spring), 33–55.

Carroll, Doug (1992), "Expert: Being on Time Isn't Everything for Airlines." *USA Today* (March 5), 6B.

Chebat, Jean-Charles, and Paul Kollias (2000), "The Impact of Empowerment on Customer Contact Employees' Roles in Service Organizations." *Journal of Service Research* 3 (1) (August), 66–81.

Chung, Beth G., and Benjamin Schneider (1999), "Correlates of Service Employees' Role Conflict." Ithaca, N.Y.: Cornell University, School of Hotel Administration, Working Paper.

Churchill, Gilbert R., Jr. (1979), "A Paradigm for Developing Better Measures of Marketing Constructs." *Journal of Marketing Research* 16 (February), 64–73.

Clemmer, Elizabeth C., and Benjamin Schneider (1993), "Toward Understanding and Controlling Customer Dissatisfaction." In *Designing a Winning Service Strategy*, eds. Mary Jo Bitner and Lawrence Crosby, 87–91. Chicago, Ill.: American Marketing Association.

Crompton, John L., and Kelly J. Mackay (1989), "Users' Perceptions of the Relative Importance of Service Quality Dimensions in Selected Public Recreation Programs." *Leisure Sciences* 11 (4), 367–75.

Cronin, J. Joseph, Jr., and Steven A. Taylor (1992), "Measuring Service Quality: A Reexamination and Extension." *Journal of Marketing* 56 (3) (July), 55–68.

Crosby, Philip B. (1979), *Quality Is Free: The Art of Making Quality Certain*. New York, N.Y.: New American Library.

Dawkins, Peter, and Frederick F. Reichheld (1990), "Customer Retention as a Strategic Weapon." *Directors and Boards* 14 (Summer), 41–7.

Dickson, Peter (1994), *Marketing Management*. Fort Worth, Tex.: Dryden Press.

Donthu, Naveen, and Boonghee Yoo (1998), "Cultural Influences on Service Quality Expectations." *Journal of Service Research* 1 (2) (November), 178–86.

Easton, George S. (1993), "The 1993 State of U.S. Total Quality Management: A Baldrige Examiner's Perspective." *California Management Review* 35 (3), 32–54.

Easton, George S., and Sherry L. Jarrell (1998), "The Effects of Total Quality Management on Corporate Performance." *Journal of Business* 71 (April), 253–308.

Economist, The (1992), "The Cracks in Quality." 18 (April), 67–8.

Ehrenfeld, Tom (1992), "The Case of the Unpopular Pay Plan." *Harvard Business Review* 70 (January-February), 14–7.

Farley, John M., Carson F. Daniels, and Daniel H. Pearl (1990), "Service Quality in a Multinational Environment." *Proceedings of the ASQC Quality Congress Transactions,* San Francisco, Calif.: American Society for Quality Control.

Finn, David W., and Charles W. Lamb, Jr. (1991), "An Evaluation of the SERVQUAL Scales in a Retail Setting." In *Advances in Consumer Research*, eds. Rebecca H. Holman and Michael R. Solomon, 18. Provo, Utah: Association for Consumer Research.

Fisher, Lawrence M. (1998), "Here Comes Front-Office Automation." *Strategy and Business* 13 (Fourth Quarter), 53–65.

Fisk, Raymond P., Stephen W. Brown, and Mary Jo Bitner (1993), "Tracking the Evolution of the Services Marketing Literature." *Journal of Retailing* 69 (Spring), 61–103.

Fitzgerald, C., and T. Erdmann (1992), *Actionline,* Newsletter for the Automotive Industry Action Group (October), 45–56.

Fitzsimmons, James A., and Mona J. Fitzsimmons (1997), *Service Management,* 2nd ed., chap. 11. New York, N.Y.: Irwin/McGraw-Hill.

Ford Motor Company (1990), "Memorandum to Dealers." (October 3).

Ford, John B., Mathew Joseph, and Beatriz Joseph (1993), "Service Quality in Higher Education: A Comparison of Universities in the United States and New Zealand Using SERVQUAL." In *Enhancing Knowledge Development in Marketing, 1993 AMA Educators' Conference Proceedings,* 75–81. Chicago, Ill.: American Marketing Association.

Fornell, Claes, Michael D. Johnson, Eugene W. Anderson, Jaesung Cha, and Barbara Everitt Bryant (1996), "The American Customer Satisfaction Index: Nature, Purpose and Findings." *Journal of Marketing* 60 (4) (October), 7–18.

Fornell, Claes, and Birger Wernerfelt (1987), "Defensive Marketing Strategy by Customer Complaint Management: A Theoretical Analysis." *Journal of Marketing Research* 24 (November), 337–46.

Fornell, Claes, and Birger Wernerfelt (1988), "A Model for Customer Complaint Management." *Marketing Science* 7 (3) (Summer), 287–98.

Furrer, Olivier, Ben Shaw-Ching Liu, and D. Sudharshan (2000), "The Relationships Between Culture and Service Quality Perceptions." *Journal of Service Research* 2 (4) (May), 355–71.

Gale, Bradley (1992), "Monitoring Customer Satisfaction and Market–Perceived Quality." *Worth Repeating Series*, No. 922CSO1. Chicago, Ill.: American Marketing Association.

Garvin, David A. (1983), "Quality on the Line." *Harvard Business Review* 61 (September-October), 65–73.

George, William R., and Leonard L. Berry (1981), "Guidelines for the Advertising of Services." *Business Horizons* 24 (May-June), 52–6.

Goodwin, Cathy (1988), "'I Can Do It Myself': Training the Service Consumer to Contribute to Service Productivity." *Journal of Services Marketing* 2 (Fall), 71–8.

Grant, Alan W., and Leonard A. Schlesinger (1995), "Realize Your Customers' Full Profit Potential." *Harvard Business Review* 73 (September-October), 59–72.

Grönroos, Christian (1982), *Strategic Management and Marketing in the Service Sector*. Helsingfors, Sweden: Swedish School of Economics and Business Administration.

Grove, Steven, and Raymond Fisk (1997), "The Impact of Other Customers on Service Experiences: A Critical Incident Examination of 'Getting Along.'" *Journal of Retailing* 73 (1) (Spring), 63–85.

Gwinner, Kevin P., Dwayne D. Gremler, and Mary Jo Bitner (1998), "Relational Benefits in Service Industries: The Customer's Perspective." *Journal of the Academy of Marketing Science* 26 (2) (Spring), 101–14.

Hartline, Michael D., and O. C. Ferrell (1996), "The Management of Customer-Contact Service Employees: An Empirical Investigation." *Journal of Marketing* 60 (4) (October), 52–70.

Harvey, Jean (1998), "Service Quality: A Tutorial." *Journal of Operations Management* 16 (5), 583–97.

Hauser, John R., Duncan I. Simester, and Birger Wernerfelt (1994), "Customer Satisfaction Incentives." *Marketing Science* 13 (4) (Fall), 327–50.

Hays, Julie M., and Arthur V. Hill (2001), "A Preliminary Investigation of the Relationships between Employee Motivation/Vision, Service Learning, and Perceived Service Quality." *Journal of Operations Management* 19 (3), 335–49.

Hendricks, Kevin B., and Vinod R. Singhal (1997), "Does Implementing an Effective TQM Program Actually Improve Operating Performance? Empirical Evidence from Firms That Have Won Quality Awards." *Management Science* 43 (9), 1258–74.

Heskett, James L., W. Earl Sasser, Jr., and Leonard A. Schlesinger (1997), *The Service Profit Chain*. New York, N.Y.: The Free Press.

Hofstede, Geert (1991), *Cultures and Organizations: Software of the Mind*. New York, N.Y.: McGraw-Hill.

International Customer Service Association (ICSA) and e–Satisfy.com (2000), http://sellitontheWeb.com/ezine/news0382.shtml (retrieved March 1, 2004).

Ittner, Christopher, and David F. Larcker (1996), "Measuring the Impact of Quality Initiatives on Firm Financial Performance." In *Advances in the Management of Organizational Quality*, eds. Soumeh Ghosh and Donald Fedor, 1–37. Greenwich, Conn.: JAI Press.

Ittner, Christopher, and David F. Larcker (1997), "The Performance Effects of Process Management Techniques." *Management Science* 43 (4), 523–34.

Johlke, Mark C., and Dale F. Duhan (2000), "Supervisor Communication Practices and Service Employee Job Outcomes." *Journal of Service Research* 3 (2) (November), 154–65.

Johnson, Linda L., Michael J. Dotson, and B. J. Dunlop (1988), "Service Quality Determinants and Effectiveness in the Real Estate Brokerage Industry." *The Journal of Real Estate Research* 3 (1), 21–36.

Katz, Daniel, and Robert L. Kahn (1978), *The Social Psychology of Organizations*. New York, N.Y.: Wiley and Sons.

Kelley, Scott W., and K. Douglas Hoffman (1997), "An Investigation of Positive Affect, Prosocial Behaviors, and Service Quality." *Journal of Retailing* 73 (3) (Fall), 407–27.

Kelley, Scott W., Steven J. Skinner, and James H. Donnelly, Jr. (1992), "Organizational Socialization of Service Customers." *Journal of Business Research* 25 (2), 197–214.

Kingman-Brundage, Jane (1991), "Technology, Design and Service Quality." *International Journal of Service Industry Management* 2 (3), 47–59.

Kordupleski, Raymond E., Roland T. Rust, and Anthony J. Zahorik (1993), "Why Improving Quality Doesn't Improve Quality (or Whatever Happened to Marketing?)." *California Management Review* 35 (3), 82–95.

Koska, Mart T. (1990), "High Quality Care and Hospital Profits: Is there a Link?" *Hospitals* (March 5), 62–3.

Legg, Donna, and Julie Baker (1991), "Advertising Strategies for Service Firms." In *Services Marketing*, ed. Christopher Lovelock, 282–91. Englewood Cliffs, N.J.: Prentice-Hall.

Lehtinen, Uolevi, and Jarmo R. Lehtinen (1982), "Service Quality: A Study of Quality Dimensions." Helsinki, Finland: Service Management Institute, Unpublished Working Paper.

Levitt, Theodore (1976), "The Industrialization of Service." *Harvard Business Review* 54 (September-October), 63–74.

Lewis, Robert C., and Bernard H. Booms (1983), "The Marketing Aspects of Service Quality." In *Emerging Perspectives on Services Marketing*, eds. Leonard L. Berry, G. Lynn Shostack, and Gregory Upah, 99–107. Chicago, Ill.: American Marketing Association.

Lociacono, Eleanor, Richard T. Watson, and Dale Goodhue (2000), "WebQual™: A Web Site Quality Instrument." Worcester, Mass.: Worcester Polytechnic Institute, Working Paper.

Mann, Robin, and Dennis Kehoe (1994), "An Evaluation of the Effects of Quality Improvement Activities on Business Performance." *The International Journal of Quality and Reliability Management* 11 (4), 29–45.

Martin, Charles I., and Charles A. Pranter (1989), "Compatibility Management: Customer-to-Customer Relationships in Service Environments." *Journal of Services Marketing* 3 (3) (Summer), 5–15.

Matthews, J., and P. Katel (1992), "The Cost of Quality: Faced with Hard Times, Business Sours on Total Quality Management." *Newsweek* (September 7), 48–9.

Mattila, Anna S. (1999), "The Role of Culture in the Service Evaluation Process." *Journal of Service Research* 1 (3), 250–61.

McLaughlin, John P. (1993), "Ensuring Customer Satisfaction Is a Strategic Issue, Not Just an Operational One." Presentation at the AIC Customer Satisfaction Measurement Conference, Chicago, December.

Mick, David Glenn, and Susan Fournier (1995), "Technological Consumer Products in Everyday Life: Ownership, Meaning, and Satisfaction." Cambridge, Mass.: Marketing Science Institute, Report No. 95–104.

Mick, David Glenn, and Susan Fournier (1998), "Paradoxes of Technology: Consumer Cognizance, Emotions, and Coping Strategies." *Journal of Consumer Research* 25 (2) (September), 123–47.

Nelson, Eugene, Roland T. Rust, Anthony Zahorik, Robin L. Rose, Paul Batalden, and Beth Siemanski (1992), "Do Patient Perceptions of Quality Relate to Hospital Financial Performance?" *Journal of Healthcare Marketing* 12 (4) (December), 1–13.

Normann, Richard (1984), *Service Management.* New York, N.Y.: John Wiley.

Nunnally, Jum C. (1978), *Psychometric Theory*, 2nd ed. New York, N.Y.: McGraw-Hill.

Ouchi, William G., and Mary Ann McGuire (1975), "A Conceptual Framework for the Design of Organizational Control Mechanisms." *Management Science* 25 (9), 833–48.

Parasuraman, A. (2000), "Technology Readiness Index (TRI): A Multiple Item Scale to Measure Readiness to Embrace New Technologies." *Journal of Service Research* 2 (4) (May), 307– 20.

Parasuraman, A., Leonard L. Berry, and Valarie A. Zeithaml (1991a), "Understanding Customer Expectations of Service." *Sloan Management Review* 32 (3) (Spring), 39–48.

Parasuraman, A., Leonard L. Berry, and Valarie A. Zeithaml (1991b), "Refinement and Reassessment of the SERVQUAL Scale." *Journal of Retailing* 67 (Winter), 420–50.

Parasuraman, A., Leonard L. Berry, and Valarie A. Zeithaml (1993), "More on Improving Service Quality Measurement." *Journal of Retailing* 69 (Spring), 40–147.

Parasuraman, A., Valarie A. Zeithaml, and Leonard L. Berry (1985), "A Conceptual Model of Service Quality and Its Implications for Future Research." *Journal of Marketing* 49 (4) (Fall), 41–50.

Parasuraman, A., Valarie A. Zeithaml, and Leonard L. Berry (1988), "SERVQUAL: A Multiple-Item Scale for Measuring Consumer Perceptions of Service Quality." *Journal of Retailing* 64 (Spring), 12–40.

Parasuraman, A., Valarie A. Zeithaml, and Leonard L. Berry (1994a), "Reassessment of Expectations as a Comparison Standard in Measuring Service Quality: Implications for Further Research." *Journal of Marketing* 58 (1) (January), 111–24.

Parasuraman, A., Valarie A. Zeithaml, and Leonard L. Berry (1994b), "Moving Forward in Service Quality Research: Measuring Different Customer-Expectation Levels, Comparing Alternative Scales, and Examining the Performance-Behavioral Intentions Link." Cambridge, Mass.: Marketing Science Institute, Report No. 94–114

Parasuraman, A., Valarie A. Zeithaml, and Arvind Malhotra (2004), "e-SERVQUAL: A Multiple–Item Scale for Assessing Electronic Service Quality." Miami, Fla.: University of Miami, Working Paper.

Perreault, William D., Jr. (1992), "The Shifting Paradigm in Marketing Research." *Journal of the Academy of Marketing Science* 20 (Fall), 367–75.

Peter, J. Paul, Gilbert A. Churchill, Jr., and Tom J. Brown (1993), "Caution in the Use of Difference Scores in Consumer Research." *Journal of Consumer Research* 19 (4) (March), 655–62.

Peters, Thomas J. (1988), *Thriving on Chaos*. New York, N.Y.: Alfred A. Knopf.

Phillips, Lynn W., Dae R. Chang, and Robert D. Buzzell (1983), "Product Quality, Cost Position, and Business Performance: A Test of Some Key Hypotheses." *Journal of Marketing* 47 (2) (Spring), 26–43.

key

Reger, Rhonda K., L. T. Gustafson, S. M. Demarie, and J. V. Mulland (1994), "Reframing the Organization: Why Implementing Total Quality Is Easier Said Than Done." *Academy of Management Review* 19 (3), 565–84.

Reichheld, Frederick (1993), "Loyalty–Based Management." *Harvard Business Review* 71 (March-April), 64–74.

Reichheld, Frederick (1996a), "Learning from Customer Defections." *Harvard Business Review* 74 (March-April), 56–69.

Reichheld, Frederick (1996b), *The Loyalty Effect: The Hidden Force Behind Growth, Profits, and Lasting Value.* Boston. Mass.: Harvard Business School Press.

Reichheld, Frederick, and W. Earl Sasser, Jr. (1990), "Zero Defections: Quality Comes to Services." *Harvard Business Review* 68 (September-October), 105–11.

Rizzo, John, R. J. House, and S. I. Lirtzman (1970), "Role Conflict and Ambiguity in Complex Organizations." *Administrative Science Quarterly* 15 (2), 150–63.

Rose, S. (1990), "The Coming Revolution in Credit Cards." *The Journal of Retail Banking* 12 (Summer), 17–9.

Rucci, Anthony J., Steven P. Kirn, and Richard T. Quinn (1998), "The Employee-Customer-Profit Chain at Sears." *Harvard Business Review* 76 (January-February), 82–97.

Rust, Roland T., Timothy Keiningham, Stephen Clemens, and Anthony Zahorik (1998), "Return on Quality at Chase Manhattan Bank." Nashville, Tenn.: Vanderbilt University, Center for Service Marketing, Working Paper.

Rust, Roland, Bala Subramanian, and Mark Wells (1992), "Making Complaints a Management Tool." *Marketing Management* 2 (3), 40–5.

Rust, Roland T., Anthony J. Zahorik, and Timothy L. Keiningham (1994), *Return on Quality* Chicago, Ill.: Probus Publishing Co.

Rust, Roland T., Anthony J. Zahorik, and Timothy L. Keiningham (1995), "Return on Quality (ROQ): Making Service Quality Financially Accountable." *Journal of Marketing* 59 (2) (April), 58–70.

Sasser, W. Earl, Jr., R. Paul Olsen, and D. Daryl Wyckoff (1978), *Management of Service Operations: Text, Cases, and Readings.* Boston, Mass.: Pearson Allyn & Bacon.

Schlesinger, Leonard A., and James L. Heskett (1991), "The Service-Driven Service Company." *Harvard Business Review* 69 (September-October), 71–81.

Schneider, Benjamin, and David E. Bowen (1985), "Employee and Customer Perceptions of Service in Banks: Replication and Extension." *Journal of Applied Psychology* 70 (3), 423–33.

Schneider, Benjamin, and David E. Bowen (1993), "The Service Organization: Human Resources Management Is Crucial." *Organizational Dynamics* 21 (4), 39–52.

Schneider, Benjamin, and David E. Bowen (1995), *Winning the Service Game*, chap. 5. Boston, Mass.: Harvard Business School Press.

Schneider, Benjamin, and Daniel Schechter (1991), "Development of a Personnel Selection System for Service Jobs." In *Service Quality: Multidisciplinary and Multinational Perspectives*, eds. Stephen W. Brown, Evert Gummesson, Bo Evardsson, and BengtOve Gustavsson, 217–36. Lexington, Mass.: Lexington Books.

Serwer, Andrew E. (1995), "Trouble in Franchise Nation." *Fortune* (March 6), 115–8.

Shostack, G. Lynn (1992), "Understanding Services Through Blueprinting." In *Advances in Services Marketing, and Management: Research and Practice*, vol. 1, eds. Teresa A. Swartz, David E. Bowen, and Stephen W. Brown, 75–90. Greenwich, Conn.: JAI Press.

Simester, Duncan I., John R. Hauser, Birger Wernerfelt, and Roland T. Rust (1998), "Implementing Quality Improvement Programs Designed to Enhance Customer Satisfaction: Quasi-Experiments in the U.S. and Spain." Cambridge, Mass.: MIT, Sloan School of Management, Working Paper.

Singh, Jagdip, Jerry R. Goolsby, and Gary K. Rhoads (1994), "Behaviorial and Psychological Consequences of Boundary Spanning: Burnout and Customer Service Representatives." *Journal of Marketing Research* 31 (November), 558–69.

Sterman, John D., Nelson P. Repenning, and Fred Kofman (1997), "Unanticipated Side Effects of Successful Quality Programs: Exploring a Paradox of Organizational Improvement." *Management Science* 43 (4), 503–21.

Szymanski, David M., and Richard T. Hise (2000), "e-Satisfaction: An Initial Examination." *Journal of Retailing* 76 (3) (Fall), 309–22.

Tax, Stephen S., and Stephen W. Brown (1998), "Recovering and Learning from Service Failure." *Sloan Management Review* 40 (1) (Fall), 75–88.

Taylor, Shirley (1994), "Waiting for Service: The Relationship between Delays and Evaluations of Service." *Journal of Marketing* 58 (2) (April), 56–69.

Teas, R. Kenneth (1993), "Expectations, Performance Evaluation, and Consumers' Perceptions of Quality." *Journal of Marketing* 57 (4) (October), 18–34.

U. S. General Accounting Office (1991), *Management Practice: U.S. Companies Improve Performance Through Quality Efforts*. Washington, D.C: U.S. General Accounting Office.

Walker, Orville C., Gilbert A. Churchill, Jr., and Neil M. Ford (1977), "Motivation and Performance in Industrial Selling: Present Knowledge and Needed Research." *Journal of Marketing Research* 14 (May), 156–68.

Webster, Frederick E., Jr. (1992), "The Changing Role of Marketing in the Corporation." *Journal of Marketing* 56 (4) (October), 1–17.

Winslow, Ron (1992), "Videos, Questionnaires Aim to Expand Role of Patients in Treatment Decisions." *The Wall Street Journal* (February 25), B1.

Winsted, Kathryn Frazier (1997), "The Service Experience in Two Cultures: A Behavioral Perspective." *Journal of Retailing* 73 (3) (Fall), 337–60.

Wolfinbarger, Mary, and Mary C. Gilly (2002), ".comQ: Dimensionalizing, Measuring, and Predicting Quality of the E-tail Experience." Cambridge, Mass.: Marketing Science Institute, Report No. 02–100.

Wolfinbarger, Mary, and Mary Gilly (2003), "e-TailQ: Dimensionalizing, Measuring and Predicting etail Quality." *Journal of Retailing* 79 (3) (Fall), 183–98.

Woodruff, Robert B., D. Scott Clemons, David W. Schumann, Sarah F. Gardial, and Mary Jane Burns (1991), "The Standards Issue in CS/D Research: A Historical Perspective." *Journal of Consumer Satisfaction, Dissatisfaction and Complaining Behavior* 4, 103–9.

Woodside, Arch G., Lisa L. Frey, and Robert Timothy Daly (1989), "Linking Service Quality, Customer Satisfaction, and Behavioral Intention." *Journal of Health Care Marketing* 9 (December), 5–17.

Zahorik, Anthony J., and Roland T. Rust (1992), "Modeling the Impact of Service Quality on Profitability: A Review." In *Advances in Service Quality and Management*, vol. 1, ed. Terry Schwartz, 247–76. Greenwich, Conn.: JAI Press.

Zeithaml, Valarie A. (1988), "Consumer Perceptions of Price, Quality, and Value: A Means-End Model and Synthesis of Research." *Journal of Marketing* 52 (3) (July), 2–22.

Zeithaml, Valarie A., Leonard L. Berry, and A. Parasuraman (1988), "Communication and Control Processes in the Delivery of Service Quality." *Journal of Marketing* 52 (2) (April), 35–48.

Zeithaml, Valarie A., Leonard L. Berry, and A. Parasuraman (1993), "The Nature and Determinants of Customer Expectations of Service." *Journal of the Academy of Marketing Science* 21 (1) (Winter), 1–12.

Zeithaml, Valarie A., Leonard L. Berry, and A. Parasuraman (1996), "The Behavioral Consequences of Service Quality." *Journal of Marketing* 60 (2) (April), 31–46.

Zeithaml, Valarie, and Mary J. Bitner (2003), *Services Marketing: Integrating Customer Focus Across the Firm*, 3rd ed. Burr Ridge, Ill.: Irwin McGraw-Hill.

Zeithaml, Valarie A., A. Parasuraman, and Leonard L. Berry (1990), *Delivering Quality Service: Balancing Customer Perceptions and Expectations*. New York, N.Y.: The Free Press.

Zeithaml, Valarie A., A. Parasuraman, and Arvind Malhotra (2000), "A Conceptual Framework for Understanding e–Service Quality: Implications for Future Research and Managerial Practice." Cambridge, Mass.: Marketing Science Institute, Report No. 00–115.

Zeithaml, Valarie A., A. Parasuraman, and Arvind Malhotra (2002), "Service Quality Delivery Through Websites: A Critical Review of Extant Knowledge." *Journal of the Academy of Marketing Science* 30 (4) (Fall), 362–75.

Zeithaml, Valarie A., Roland T. Rust, and Katherine N. Lemon (2001), "The Customer Pyramid: Creating and Servicing Profitable Customers." *California Management Review* 43 (4), 2001.

ABOUT THE AUTHORS

Valarie A. Zeithaml

Valarie A. Zeithaml is the Roy and Alice H. Richards Bicentennial Professor and MBA Associate Dean at the Kenan-Flagler Business School of the University of North Carolina, Chapel Hill.

Since receiving her MBA and Ph.D. in marketing from the Robert H. Smith School of Business at the University of Maryland in 1980, Professor Zeithaml has devoted her career to researching and teaching the topics of service quality and services management. She is the author of three books: *Delivery Quality Service: Balancing Customer Perceptions and Expectations* (with A. Parasuraman and Leonard L. Berry, The Free Press, 1990), now in its thirteenth printing; *Driving Customer Equity: How Customer Lifetime Value Is Reshaping Corporate Strategy* (with Roland Rust and Katherine Lemon, The Free Press, 2000); and *Services Marketing: Integrating Customer Focus across the Firm* (with Mary Jo Bitner, McGraw-Hill/Irwin, 2003), a textbook now in its third edition. In 2002, *Driving Customer Equity* won the first Berry-American Marketing Association Book Prize for the best marketing book of the past three years.

In 2004, Professor Zeithaml received both the Innovative Contributor to Marketing Award, given by the Marketing Management Association, and the Outstanding Marketing Educator Award, given by the Academy of Marketing Science. In 2001, she received the American Marketing Association's Career Contributions to the Services Discipline Award.

Professor Zeithaml has won five teaching awards, including the Gerald Barrett Faculty Award from the University of North Carolina and The Fuqua School Outstanding MBA Teaching Award from Duke University. She is also the recipient of numerous research awards, including the Robert Ferber Consumer Research Award from the *Journal of Consumer Research*, the Harold H. Maynard Award from the *Journal of Marketing*, the Jagdish Sheth Award from the *Journal of the Academy of Marketing Science*, and the William F. O'Dell Award from the *Journal of Marketing Research*. She has consulted with over 50 service and product companies.

Professor Zeithaml served on the Board of Directors of the American Marketing Association from 2000 to 2003 and is currently an Academic Trustee of the Marketing Science Institute.

A. Parasuraman

A. Parasuraman ("Parsu") is a Professor and Holder of the James W. McLamore Chair in Marketing, endowed by the Burger King Corporation, at the University of Miami. He obtained his B. Tech. from I.I.T.-Madras (India) in 1970 and his MBA from I.I.M.-Ahmedabad (India) in 1972. He received his DBA in 1975 from Indiana University.

In 1988 Professor Parasuraman was selected as one of the "Ten Most Influential Figures in Quality" by the editorial board of *The Quality Review*, co-published by the American Quality Foundation and the American Society for Quality Control. He has received many distinguished teaching and research awards, including many "Best Professor" awards given by EMBA classes and the Provost's Award for Scholarly Research at the University of Miami. In 1998 he received the American Marketing Association's Career Contributions to the Services Discipline Award. In 2001, he received the Academy of Marketing Science's Outstanding Marketing Educator Award.

Professor Parasuraman has written numerous articles in journals such as the *Journal of Marketing, Journal of Marketing Research, Journal of the Academy of Marketing Science, Journal of Retailing,* and *Sloan Management Review.* He served as editor of the *Journal of the Academy of Marketing Science (JAMS)* from 1997 to 2000 and currently serves on the editorial review boards of ten journals. In 2003, he received the *JAMS* Outstanding Reviewer Award for 2000–03.

Professor Parasuraman is the lead author of a college textbook, *Marketing Research* (with Dhruv Grewal and R. Krishnan, Houghton Mifflin, 2003), and is a co-author of three business books written for practitioners: *Delivering Quality Service: Balancing Customer Perceptions and Expectations* (with Valarie Zeithaml and Leonard L. Berry, The Free Press, 1990), *Marketing Services: Competing Through Quality* (with Leonard L. Berry, Free Press, 1991), and *Techno-Ready Marketing: How and Why Your Customers Adopt Technology* (with Charles L. Colby, The Free Press, 2001). He has conducted dozens of executive seminars on service quality, customer satisfaction, and the role of technology in service delivery in many countries.

ABOUT MSI

The Marketing Science Institute connects businesspeople and academic researchers who are committed to advancing the theory and practice of marketing in order to achieve higher levels of business performance. Founded in 1961, MSI currently brings together executives from approximately 65 sponsoring corporations with leading researchers from over 100 universities worldwide.

As a nonprofit institution, MSI financially supports academic research for the development—and practical translation—of leading-edge marketing knowledge on topics of importance to business. Issues of key importance to business performance are identified by the Board of Trustees, which represents MSI corporations and the academic community. MSI supports studies by academics on these issues and disseminates the results through conferences and workshops, as well as through its publications series.

Related MSI Working Papers

MSI has published a number of working papers on the topic of service quality. These include:

03–107 "Online Channel Use and Satisfaction in a Multichannel Service Context" by Mitzi Montoya-Weiss, Glenn B. Voss, and Dhruv Grewal

03–104 "Ten Lessons for Improving Service Quality" by Leonard L. Berry, A. Parasuraman, and Valarie A. Zeithaml

03–101 "Creating a Superior Customer-Relating Capability" by George S. Day

02–123 "Superiority in Customer Relationship Management: Consequences for Competitive Advantage and Performance" by George S. Day and Christophe Van den Bulte

02–112 "Customer Relationship Management: Strategies and Company-wide Implementation" conference summary by Mauricio Mittelman and Vincent Onyemah

02–101 "Customer Relationship Management: Customer Behavior, Organizational Challenges, and Econometric Models" conference summary by Julian Villanueva and Rex Du

02–100 ".comQ: Dimensionalizing, Measuring, and Predicting Quality of the E-tail Experience" by Mary Wolfinbarger and Mary C. Gilly

01–116 "Consumer Trust, Value, and Loyalty in Relational Exchanges" by Deepak Sirdeshmukh, Jagdip Singh, and Barry Sabol

01–122 "Marketing to and Serving Customers Through the Internet" George Zinkhan, editor, conference summary by Kishore Gopalakrishna Pillai, Melanie Provost, and Yue Pan

96–100 "Developing Customers, Products, and Markets for Services" conference summary by Thomas Burnham

95–113 "Prepurchase Preference and Postconsumption Satisfaction in a Service Exchange" by Glenn B. Voss and A. Parasuraman

94–114 "Moving Forward in Service Quality Research: Measuring Different Customer-Expectation Levels, Comparing Alternative Scales, and Examining the Performance-Behavioral Intentions Link" by A. Parasuraman, Valarie A. Zeithaml, and Leonard L. Berry

94–106 "Return on Quality (ROQ): Making Service Quality Financially Accountable" by Roland T. Rust, Anthony J. Zahorik, and Timothy L. Keiningham

94–105 "Using Information Technology to Reduce Coordination Breakdowns in Customer Support Teams" by Sukumar Rathnam, Vijay Mahajan, and Andrew B. Whinston

93–122 "Service Quality Implementation: The Effects of Organizational Socialization and Managerial Actions on Customer-Contact Employee Behaviors" by Michael D. Hartline and O. C. Ferrell

93–108 "Development and Validation of the Corporate Social Style Inventory: A Measure of Customer Service Skills" by Juan I. Sanchez and Scott L. Fraser

93–104 "Ten Lessons For Improving Service Quality" by Leonard L. Berry, A. Parasuraman, and Valarie A. Zeithaml

92–121 "Conceptualizing and Testing a Dynamic Process Model of Service Quality" by William Boulding, Richard Staelin, Ajay Kalra, and Valarie A. Zeithaml

91–113 "The Nature and Determinants of Customer Expectations of Service" by Valarie Zeithaml, Leonard L. Berry, and A. Parasuraman

90–122 "An Empirical Examination of Relationships in an Extended Service Quality Model" by A Parasuraman, Leonard L. Berry, and Valarie A. Zeithaml

90–105 "The Effects of Perceived Control and Customer Crowding on the Service Experience" by John E. G. Bateson and Michael K. M. Hui

To order publications, visit the Publications section of *www.msi.org* or contact *pubs@msi.org*.

Meubles _ pour   150 E —
      3h bibtecs